# Third Way Allegiance

# Third Way Allegiance

*Christian Witness in the Shadow of Religious Empire*

Tripp York

Discussion Questions by Chuck Seay
Foreword by Matt Litton

Publishing House
Telford, Pennsylvania

**Cascadia Publishing House LLC orders, information, reprint permissions:**
*contact@cascadiapublishinghouse.com*
1-215-723-9125
126 Klingerman Road, Telford PA 18969
www.CascadiaPublishingHouse.com

*Third Way Allegiance*

Library of Congress Catalog Number: 2011000256
**ISBN 13:** 978-1-931038-82-9; **ISBN 10:** 1-931038-82-1
Book design by Cascadia Publishing House
Cover design by Merrill R. Miller

The paper used in this publication is recycled and meets the minimum requirements of American National Standard for Information Sciences—Permanence of Paper for Printed Library Materials, ANSI Z39.48-1984.



**Library of Congress Cataloguing-in-Publication Data**
York, Tripp.
Third way allegiance : Christian witness in the shadow of religious empire / Tripp York.
p. cm.
ISBN-13: 978-1-931038-82-9 (trade pbk. : alk. paper)
ISBN-10: 1-931038-82-1 (trade pbk. : alk. paper)
1. Church and state--United States. 2. Church and the world. 3. Theology. I. Title.
BR516.Y67 2011
261.70973--dc22
2011000256

20 19 18 17 16 15 13 12 11 10 9 8 7 6 5 4 3 2 1

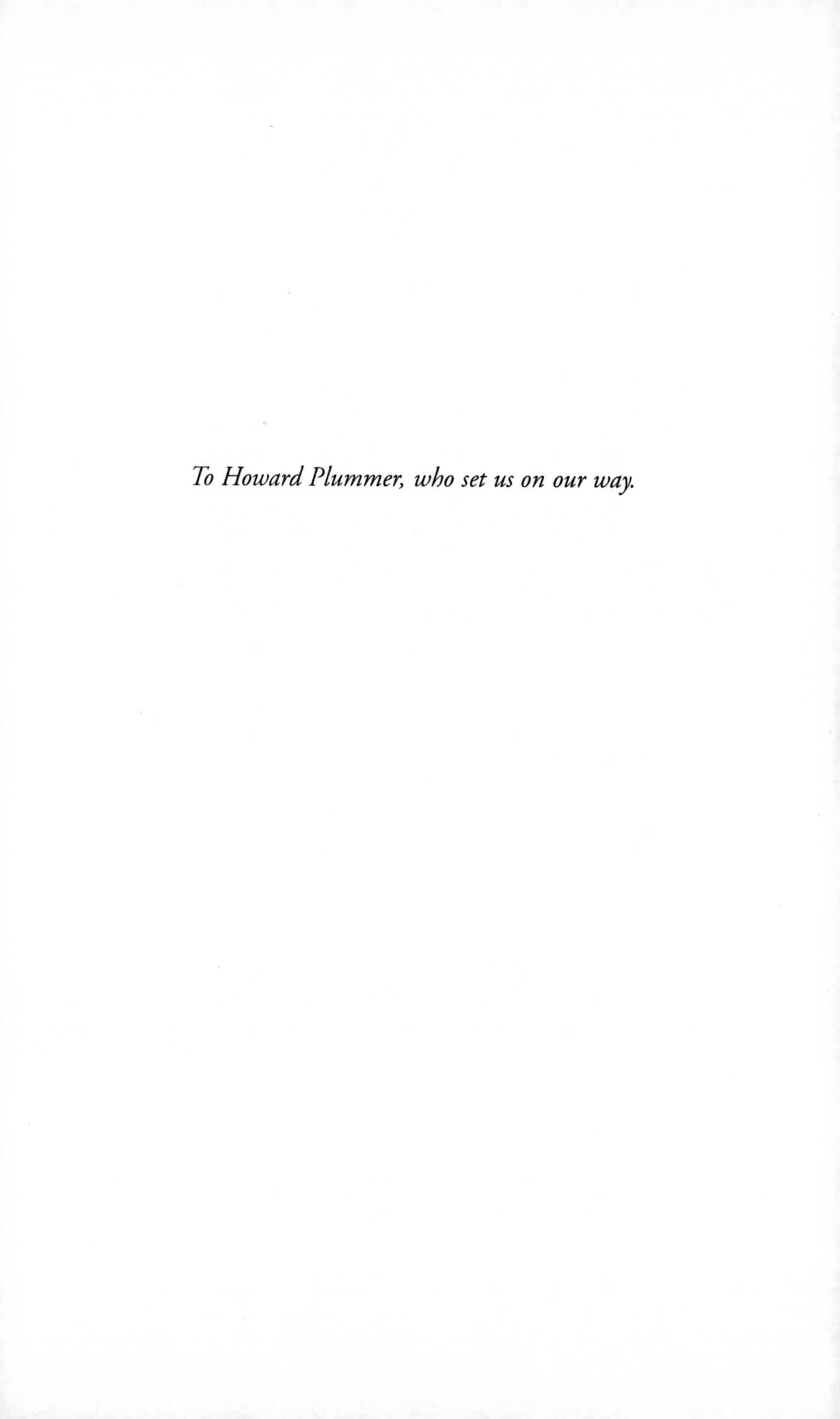

*To Howard Plummer, who set us on our way.*

# Contents

## Part III—Our Praise

# Foreword

**OUR DEVOTION** to the Christian life is often reflected in the frequency and voracity of the questions we are willing to ask regarding our faith. Becoming God's people as embodied by Jacob, who wrestled with God through the night, is the quintessential metaphor for a vibrant life of genuine discipleship. At this point in my faith journey, I am drawn to those who encourage me to ask the tough questions about what following Jesus means in my world. Tripp York inspires me accordingly.

The idea that our faith has been co-opted, in some measure, by our profound sense of loyalty to our nation (and our economics) is something that needs to be examined and reexamined. We must be reminded that the values of our politics are often at odds with the values of God's kingdom.

The gospel is bigger than our nationalism; it transcends languages, borders, and political philosophies. Yet the expression of our faith does not always reflect a genuine allegiance to the gospel of the crucified Christ. As followers of Jesus, Tripp York asks us to question our true allegiance, to examine our discipleship, and to rediscover what it means to be indentured to Jesus' kingdom vision—to be people who *hunger* and *thirst* for justice.

York's book reads like Letters to the American Church. In *Third Way Allegiance,* he examines three aspects of Western

Christianity through essays that focus on the practice, politics, and worship expressions of our faith. He challenges his readers: Is the church narrating what it means to be an American or is America narrating what it means to be the church? He calls American Christians back to the "subversion" of grace and nonviolence and assures us that "obedience is never without effect." He argues that our *lifestyles* (more than our words) should put the scandal back in discourse about God, reminds us that Christianity is not philosophically defensible, and points us back to the ideas of third-century Christians who claimed, "I believe because it is absurd."

Readers will be particularly moved by York's references to modern-day saints: the people who, in his words, "help us understand the truths of Scripture with their lives." People like Clarence Jordan, whose passion for racial equality and communal life in Georgia eventually birthed Habitat for Humanity; Dorothy Day, who began the Catholic Worker Movement as an advocate for the poor; and my favorite, Steve Irwin (yes, the Crocodile Hunter), who York believes embodies passion for creation and whose appetite for work has much to teach us about God's redemptive movement. York writes with pop-culture savvy, a strong command of theology and Scripture, and a respect for church history which readers will find poignant and accessible.

York's engaging message is anything but tame. Even when I don't agree with him, I am always challenged by his ideas. His thoughtful (and sometimes controversial) views will draw you into meaningful reflection about how your faith can be expressed in a truer, more radical way. This is certainly a book that every professor, layperson, pastor, and student should read. I believe Tripp York's call to a different type of allegiance is something that can transform your faith in a powerful way; it certainly has mine. I invite you to turn the page with me, begin the wrestling match, and embark on your journey of allegiance to the gospel of Jesus.

—*Matt Litton, Author,* The Mockingbird Parables: Transforming Lives through the Power of Story

# Acknowledgments

**LET ME BEGIN** by saying that the Mennonites and Nazarenes are to blame for much of the content of this book. I understand this is hardly a ringing endorsement for either group, but it needed to be said. This is not to suggest, of course, that there is any one monolithic thing called "Mennonite" or "Nazarene." The diversity between these two groups, as well as among themselves, is staggering and, sometimes, surprising. I find that to be, on most days, a good thing.

When I claim that these ecclesial traditions are to blame for the following arguments, I am simply giving credit to those two groups who have nurtured me within the Christian tradition. They will be relieved to know that I am not holding either one accountable for the claims made in this manuscript. I am sure that many Mennonites and Nazarenes would quickly distance themselves from a number of theological points made within these pages. I am only expressing gratitude for their providing me with the kind of resources necessary to enable me to make any theological points at all.

As the reader will see, however, I owe a debt to more than just the Mennonites and the Nazarenes. I graduated from two Methodist schools that were filled with professors significantly influenced by Catholicism. I hope such ecclesial eclecticism has served to make these arguments not just interesting but faithful to the overarching vision of the universal church. The Christian tradition is ripe with a number of divergent understandings of what it means to practice this odd thing initially referred to as "the Way" (Acts 9:2), and I hope these chapters provide at least some indication of such diversity.

As I finish this book I am wrapping up my fifth year teaching at Elon University in Elon, North Carolina. I am very grateful to all of my colleagues in the Religion Department, and I am in particular debt to both Jim Pace and Jeff Pugh for keeping me busy. My stomach and my bookshelves thank you.

It has been a real joy working with Chuck Seay. His pastoral insights have proven to be extremely helpful in the writing of this manuscript. If there are parts of this book that do not make sense, I am sure that, at some point, he told me about them. I trust that his very apt study guide makes this a more coherent book than what it would be without it.

I owe an extended debt of gratitude to Lesley Tkaczyk for her careful proofing of an earlier manuscript, and I am, once again, indebted to Maggie Pahos for her meticulous work on the index. This book would not have been possible without their keen insight and helpful suggestions.

I am especially appreciative of the work that Michael A. King is doing with Cascadia Publishing House LLC, and I am grateful for his adoption of this project. Books are always a risk, and I thank him for risking this one on me. As always, many thanks to my family (especially my sister Cherie, who took the time to comment on some of these chapters) for their continued support, and to my Tatiana whose generosity continues, to paraphrase McCartney, to amaze me.

—*Tripp York*
*Bowling Green, Kentucky*

# Author's Preface

*Our disobedience is not that we are so irreligious, but that we are so very glad to be religious . . . very relieved when some government proclaims the Christian worldview . . . so that the more pious we are, the less we let ourselves be told that God is dangerous, that God will not be mocked.*
—Dietrich Bonhoeffer

**THE CHAPTERS** that follow, some previously published, are directed toward lay readers. None of these chapters were published in anything other than Christian magazines emphasizing the life of the local church. I have found gratification in publication through other venues, such as refereed journals and books, though primarily in the sense of contributing to the academy with the hope it will trickle down into our faith communities. Such is the politics of finding (and keeping) a job in the academy. Publishing in magazines written by the church for the church, however, has brought me the most satisfaction as my call is, primarily, to the church.

For the most part, there is a common theme among these articles. Each chapter, save for two or three, attempts to think about life as a Christian under the post-Christian, yet exceptionally religious, empire that is the United States of America. I have found that such religiosity, as practiced in the U.S., often renders faithful Christian discernment difficult, as being a Christian becomes almost synonymous with being an "American." (I use that term loosely as I am only referring, in this case, to U.S. citizenship.) At times, it is quite complicated to separate who is doing the narrating: Is the church narrating what it means to be an American, or is America narrating what it means to be the church? It is not always easy to know.

Although I'm not so audacious as to think I can answer these questions, I hope these chapters shed light on how difficult it is to always know who is doing the naming. This is of paramount importance, as such naming shapes how we think about a host of issues. For example, in the following pages I attempt to speak about issues ranging from race to war, from belief to animals, in a way that reveals a commitment to the body-politic predicated on the resurrection of Jesus. Too often, I worry, our way of discussing such issues is more in line with that of common opinion (which can vary from side to side) than from any honest appraisal of believing that a first-century Jewish man was really the incarnation of God.

Ultimately, these chapters merely strive to be both faithful and provocative in terms of where Christianity has been and who Christians are called to be. In terms of faithfulness, I require a body of believers willing to hold me accountable to those things that I hold to be true. That means I must be open to their correction—hence the publishing of these thoughts.

By wishing to be provocative, I mean two things: First, discipleship, and I hope this does not come as a surprise, should not be boring! Whatever form discipleship takes, it will be at odds with a world that wants to plug us in to its way of doing things. Second, the fact that we follow a crucified God, a criminal executed in accordance with the law, suggests that discourse about this God will be provocative—perhaps even scandalous. Thus if any of this book seems outrageous or offensive, I hope the reader will be patient with me. My writing does demand correction, even as it may just possibly be corrective. Tradition is, after all, an ongoing argument, and I hope we Christians can remain faithful with regard to the *kind* of arguments that end up constituting us as a people.

PART I

# Our People

## Introduction: Can I get a Witness?

*There are no final proofs for the existence of God, only witnesses.*
—Abraham J. Heschel

**AN AREA** of significant concern within the church and her seminaries has recently revolved around issues of faith and reason. Due to the current explosion of popular literature within the realm of atheism and agnosticism, coupled often mistakenly with "real" science, Christians have frequently found themselves exercising a defensive posture. Popular writers such as Sam Harris, Richard Dawkins, and Christopher Hitchens have all not only written extensively on the "irrational" beliefs that make up religious faith but have also enjoyed pointing out particular vices within the history of Christianity (and other religions as well).[1]

On one hand, I think there is much to learn from these writers. As Christians, we must own up to our mistakes and beg forgiveness for our transgressions. It does not matter who points it out, we must admit fault and seek reconciliation by placing ourselves, vulnerably, within the hands of those we have wronged. In terms of the "unreasonable faith" Christians are accused of maintaining, I also agree that it is us, not the unbelievers, who bear the burden of proof. That is to say, it is not up to the nonbelievers to prove the nonexistence of something; rather, it is up to those of us who believe to provide evidence for the existence of what it is we claim to believe. It is up to us to reveal the particularities of our faith convictions, and I think we do that best through our lives and not primarily through appeals to theoretical or philosophical "proofs."

The problem with philosophical proofs for the existence of God is that they give no specific content of the *kind* of God that is, supposedly, being proved. To go one step further, it may be that our very attempt to defend Christianity, ironically, leads to its very demise. Christianity is simply not philosophically defensible. It is, as St. Paul claims, foolishness to the Greeks (1 Cor. 1:23). This is not to say that philosophy is bad, for there is nothing wrong with the love of wisdom; it is just that evidence for the existence of God can only take the shape of those who claim to know this God.

True, there are many philosophical arguments for the existence of God. Some of these include St. Anselm's baffling yet riveting ontological argument, St. Aquinas' cosmological argument, and the most recent and very popular argument from design (Intelligent Design). Though many people may find these arguments to be compelling, I fear they do not accomplish the work they set out to do. Anselm and Aquinas already believed in the existence of God before establishing their arguments. They did not need these arguments for belief, for if you can prove something then you no longer require belief or faith. They simply wanted to reconcile their intellect with their faith, or to quote the eleventh-century Archbishop St. Anselm: *fides quarens intellectum*—faith seeking understanding of itself.

In a sense, the early and medieval Christians did not really see a disparity between their faith and reason, for Christian faith is but another way of seeing the world. It is its own manner of reasoning. The working out of these arguments, therefore, was never meant to take the place of faith itself. They were even understood to be problematic by the very people who wrote them because God is, ultimately, unknowable. God's transcendence cannot be domesticated by a philosophical formula. Even if these arguments were to convince us that God exists, they can only prove that a higher being of some sort—not necessarily the God of Abraham, Jacob, and Jesus—exists. These arguments tell us nothing about the actual characteristics of God, and, I think, we must therefore agree with the good Rabbi Heschel when he claims that the best evidence for the existence of God is the way we live our lives.

Unfortunately, as folks like Harris and Dawkins continually point out, it works both ways. The importance of this section, therefore, is to highlight a few individuals who lived the kind of lives that would be unintelligible if God does not exist. It is a question we must ask ourselves: If God was proven to not exist, would we actually live our lives any differently? Other than being saddened by this prospect, would our day-to-day activities actually change, or do we live lives of quiet methodical atheism—believers when we speak, yet atheists in our actions?

The first couple of articles in this section, therefore, express agreement with those atheists who suggest that our beliefs are not what the world deems logically coherent. Though I do not think there is any one monolithic thing called "reason" by which "rational" humans inherently conduct verifiably logical thinking, I do understand that most religious commitments require the kind of faith that goes beyond that which we can empirically prove. Rather than attempt to deny this, I will try to celebrate it in the first few chapters.

The remaining chapters in this section, as well as several others throughout the book, are exercises in Christian biography. I just cannot find better ways of expressing the truth of Christianity except through the lives of its believers. I should, however, point out that in this section I include a person whose faith commitments I know little about. My inclusion of Steve Irwin, also known as the Crocodile Hunter, was intentional, as I find his understanding of our gifts, in the form of our work, to this world instructive for Christians. He taught us about the goodness of both creation and work and placed it in the service of something beyond our own selves. His inclusion in this book is a healthy reminder that the so-called distinction between the sacred and the secular is not always clear. I also discuss Irwin because I fear that for all of our consideration given, and rightly so, to issues of environmentalism, we continue to neglect a key component of the environment: nonhuman animals. It is for this reason that both chapters two and three focus on our relationship with non-human animals.

Following Irwin, I discuss more confessional Christians, including a Southern Baptist whose approach to race relations necessitated the practice of farming as well as two women from different centuries both deemed ineffectual by the powers-that-be. The one thing that all three of these

Christians have in common is that both the church and the state made it a point to persecute and ridicule these individuals.

I conclude this section with a discussion of a number of people from different religious backgrounds attempting to enact a faithful witness to their understanding of God. By concluding the section with a discussion on the difference between madness and martyrdom, I hope to show how easy it is to confuse our understandings of God's will with our will—for I think the most dangerous kind of religiosity is the kind that imagines, carte blanche, that God endorses our projects.

*Chapter One*

# How Absurd is Your Christianity?

*The encounter with Jesus is fundamentally different from that with Goethe or Socrates. . . . There are only two ways possible of encountering Jesus: man must die or he must put Jesus to death.*
—Dietrich Bonhoeffer

**IN HIS TREATISE** *On the Flesh of Christ*, the third-century theologian Tertullian infamously stated that "the Son of God died; it is by all means to be believed, because it is absurd. And he was buried and rose again; the fact is certain, because it is impossible."[2] These few sentences have been popularly reduced to the Latin maxim *credo quia absurdum*: "I believe because it is absurd." Once embraced by the church as representative of the peculiarity and precariousness of Christianity, such a sentiment has now become an embarrassment to much of the Christian world. We constantly engage in the exercise of Christian apologetics to defend the "reasonableness" of our beliefs. Those reasonable beliefs include the following:

- God is three but also one;
- the second person of the triune God became incarnate in a first-century Jewish man who—
- was born of a virgin;

- turned water into wine;
- walked on water (and through walls);
- disappeared into thin air;
- cast demons into pigs who then committed suicide;
- fed thousands of people with a few loaves of bread and fish;
- brought the dead back to life;
- healed a blind man (albeit with two tries);
- healed a woman through the fabric of his robe;
- rebuked the wind and the sea (they listened);
- paid taxes by catching fish with money in its mouth, and, among many, many other things;
- was killed himself only to rise again to guarantee all those that believe in his resurrection eternal life.

Such beliefs do not exactly speak to the best of human reason and sanity. If any one person believed these things, we would consider them insane, yet because large numbers believe it, it must be true.

I am not insinuating that any of this is false; I am just saying that none of it is self-evident. There is not a statement above that is empirically verifiable; outside an unusually good ophthalmologist, I doubt anyone reading this has ever been privy to a first-hand experience that includes resurrection, suicidal pigs, and human parthenogenesis (the ability for females to become pregnant without male insemination).[3] Again, this does not render any of this false, only highly improbable. I guess that is what makes faith "faith."

Of course, as I stated in the introduction, I do not think there is any such monolithic thing known as reason or rationality; rather there are competing and rival rationalities. This does not, however, let Christians, with our very strange beliefs, off the hook. Nor should it. The one thing I have in common with many atheists is my weariness with Christians struggling so hard to make Christianity a simple matter of common sense—as if a person would be crazy *not* to believe these things.

I am simply not convinced that we can ever domesticate the peculiarity of the story of Jesus—this person who is fully divine and fully human, was killed, descended into hell, rose again, and then ascended into heaven where he has always been (even before the creation of time)—into a matter of common sense. I think everything about this story goes in the opposite direction of what is generally considered to be common sense. I also think this is a good thing.

Christianity is incorrigibly absurd. Everything about it is so incongruent with the way the world seems to work that we have to almost laugh with incredulity. After all, "God decided, through the foolishness of our proclamation, to save those who believe" (1 Cor. 1:21). If our beliefs really are "foolishness to the Greeks," then do we not deny such foolishness, such scandal, when we attempt to render our beliefs and practices comprehensible to any so-called rational mind?

Granted, I do think we owe anyone with questions as to the content of our faith an answer; I do not, however, expect it to be an answer that a non-Christian can naturally assent to or immediately understand. But that *is* the point. The content of Christianity should be different. It should also be very difficult to understand. If it is not, then I worry that we have yet to fully understand how odd and strange the content of our faith really is. After all, Christianity claims that it is we who killed the second person of the one God who is triune. Yet it was the obedience of Jesus to the Father, this Jesus who freely handed his life over to us, who was buried and, yet rose again, that made and makes possible the redemption of all creation.

Tertullian was right. It must be true, because it is simply not possible. The only thing required for us to do is to live lives based on this impossible truth so that others can revel in the absurdity of Christianity, too. Let us not give others something they can agree with but something so shockingly unusual and weird that they cannot but find it compelling. Let us show them a crucified yet resurrected Jesus.

## Discussion Questions

Why do we feel so compelled to defend the "reasonableness" of our faith? Should we not give some sort of an account that is intelligible to the non-believer? Could our defense lie more in our actions than our words?

York claims that Christianity "should also be very difficult to understand." Do you agree? Why or why not? Are there elements about Christian belief/faith/practice that should be easy or are easy? What is so difficult about Christianity?

The Anglican theologian John Milbank claims that the task of Christian theology is

> to tell again the Christian mythos, pronounce again the Christian logos and call again the Christian praxis in a manner that restores their freshness and originality. It must articulate Christian difference in such a fashion as to make it strange.[4]

York would certainly agree that the "Christian difference" should make us look strange, but how so? What makes us so different, so strange, and what should that actually look like?

*Chapter Two*

# CHRISTIANITY IS FOR THE BIRDS

*Human beings and animals shall be covered with sackcloth, and they shall cry mightily to God.*
—Jonah 3:8

**ONCE WHILE** St. Francis of Assisi was sick, a friend from Siena sent him a pheasant. Francis was grateful, not because he wished to eat the bird, but "in the way he always rejoiced over such things, out of love for the Creator."[5] Francis was ever delighted at the sight of any creatures because all, for Francis, were manifestations of God's creative wisdom. Upon the arrival of the pheasant he said, "May our Creator be praised, brother pheasant!" and then offered it the freedom to leave.[6]

When the bird chose to stay, Francis thought it wise to send it away so that it might choose a more suitable home. Yet when a brother did this, the bird returned to Francis. Francis ordered that the bird be taken farther away in hopes that it would want to stay among its own species. Again, the bird returned. This pleased Francis, so he fed the bird and offered it a home among the Franciscans. The bird had found its home.

In the previous chapter, I concluded with the suggestion that we must make visible the crucifixion and resurrection of Jesus in our own lives if we are to be faithful to that we hold true. Yet what does this look like? Granted, it can manifest itself in a wide variety of shapes, as there is no one fixed manner in which Christian witness must be embodied. Countless Christians died at the stake, in the mouths of beasts, and on the racks because of their faith. Others challenged emperors, monarchs, dictators, and presidents due to their commitment to the Jewish messiah Jesus. Some held the hands of dying lepers, some took the place of others in concentration camps, while one person in particular, St. Francis of Assisi, preached to birds (as well as crickets, bees, and wolves).

This may strike some of us as very odd behavior, perhaps even a bit crazy. Christopher Hitchens, author of the best-selling book *God Is Not Great*, is one such person. He finds such behavior to be incredibly perplexing.[7] He is even more perplexed—quite delighted and amused actually—that most Christians appear oblivious to the fact that Francis did indeed preach and demand the conversion of animals. Hitchens casually dismisses Francis as being certifiably insane (along with those who named him a saint). That the church would call, in the mind of Hitchens, such an obvious candidate for the insane asylum a saint is further evidence that Christianity really is, according to Hitchens, utterly ridiculous.[8]

Yet Jesus did say to preach to all creation (Mark 16:15), and it seems that one of the reasons God wanted Jonah to preach to the Ninevites was due to God's concern for all animals (Jonah 4:11). After all, if "all animals belong to God" (Ps. 24:1) and God cares for all animals (1 John 4:16), then why should we be shocked to find Christians concerned for the well-being of nonhuman animals?

The problem, I imagine, stems from the notion that animals, other than human animals, can somehow repent and, therefore, convert. Perhaps. But what if such an idea has more to do with the poverty of our imagination than a faithful understanding of the redemption of all creation? Though most will suggest that for instance, dogs, pheasants, or marmosets are not included in salvation history because they do not have souls, we must ask, What does the presence of a soul matter for Christians, given that our hope lies not in the immortality of the soul but in bodily resurrection? If God's peaceable kingdom includes the vision of Isaiah 11, where all creatures are included on God's heavenly mountain, then is it really so strange that somewhere along the line a few devout Christians took it upon themselves to treat other creatures as of worth to the God who loves all creatures?

Though I do not think this requires most of us to take our ministries to the woods, prairies, and deserts (as far more interesting as that would be in comparison to most church marketing strategies), it does require us to remember that there is nothing crazy about love for anything God has created. Yes, Francis conversed with, and preached to, crickets, birds, bees, and wolves. He would often speak to these creatures and ask that the cricket sing the glories of God, that the falcon awaken him in time for his religious duties, and that wolves attempt to live in harmony with humans. He referred to these creatures as his brother and sisters. Why? Because the one sure thing he knew he had in common with crickets, birds, bees, and wolves was a common creator. This was the same creator who proclaimed all creation good and demanded that humans care for God's good creation. Francis should not be belittled because he preached to birds; rather, we should be reprimanded for forgetting that Christianity is, also, for the birds.

## Discussion Questions

What are ways we can actually preach to all of creation? Do you think this has to be confined to the verbal? Are there ways in which we preach to creation by how we treat the earth and all that is in it?

Why do you think some people assume that a person like St. Francis is crazy? Do you think Francis is crazy? Is it that difficult to imagine that people who take seriously the path of Jesus might find themselves labeled "insane"?

There is much language in Scripture depicting animals and humans living together and both being under the watchful care of God. Why does this matter for how we imagine the place that animals have in God's redemption of the world?

*Chapter Three*

# The Theological Significance of One Strange Australian

*But ask the animals, and they will tell you, the birds of the air, and they will tell you, ask the plants of the earth, and they will teach you, and fish of the sea will declare to you. Who among all these does not know that the hand of the Lord has done this? In his hand is the life of every living thing and the breath of every human being.*
—Job 12:7-10

**STEVE IRWIN**, internationally known as the "Crocodile Hunter," was killed by a stingray on September 4, 2006. Despite the fact that fans and non-fans alike had been predicting his demise for some time (how long can one tempt the leviathan without a bit of bad luck?), his death came as a shock. Probably most shocking was the way he was killed: impaled through the chest by a non-aggressive creature that has claimed, barely, a handful of people in the Australian waters. There is nothing amusing in such irony.

I must first admit that I know nothing of Irwin's faith commitments, if he had any, or if he did, its content. I do know that he mentioned God on more than one occasion on his show, and he did so in reference to both his gift with animals and the goodness of creation. I also know, as a long-time fan of his TV show and his work as a wildlife conservationist, that he had a genuine love for his work and for God's creation. For this reason, as Christians, the meaning of his life deserves reflection.

In an interview two years prior to his death, Irwin was asked what he wanted to be most remembered for. "Passion and enthusiasm," he replied. If anyone ever paid more than thirty seconds worth of attention to Irwin, they recognized that he was not short on either. Because of his love for his work, Irwin often appeared borderline strange. How many of us can say that we approach our jobs with the same kind of love and purposefulness as the crocodile hunter?

Yet he did, and I imagine that part of that has to do with the fact that work, for him, was vocational. Irwin once said he felt he was put on this earth with a specific mission (as he would say we all are), and his task was the preservation of wildlife. This was his calling, and he attacked it with the kind of fervor that made even the most disinterested viewer less apathetic. In this regard, Irwin has made me question my passion for my own work—which is that of a professor of religious studies. I do enjoy it, but even before his death it was because of him that I had become far more reflective on the fact that, if this is what I am called to do, then how is the calling itself shown in *how* I work?

Work is what most of us spend the majority of our lives engaged in, and I imagine that most of us desire such work, that which is essentially our lives, to be meaningful. I cannot help but think that the way in which we perform such work, especially in the sense of whether or not we have thought well about how such work is or is not vocational, reveals to others what it is we think about our own calling in life and how this does or does not reflect the goodness of God. That is, do we love what we do, and does what we do, and how we do it, reflect who we are as Christians? As a body of people charged with the mission of making Jesus visible to the non-ecclesial world, does what we spend the majority of our lives doing reflect one of the central claims of Christianity that creation, despite its fallen-ness, is good and, because of its fallenness, continues to groan for completion (Rom. 8:22-23)?

In relation to this, I find this particular aspect of Irwin's life to be of the greatest significance. His life was, in many ways (intentionally or not), an eschatological witness to the way the world was created, was meant to be, and will one day once again be. He did not treat non-human animals the way many animal rights advocates desire: that is simply leaving them to their own devices. Rather, he took a more biblical approach in that he recognized non-human animals as not only our kin but our covenant partners (in terms of the Noahic covenant).

He did not simply let creatures be; rather, he intervened on their behalf because he recognized the beauty, the goodness, and the mystery that is found within all of creation. He saw these animals as fellow creatures that, precisely because they are under our domain, desperately require our care. For what kind of Christian could ever be indifferent to the possible eradication of any species? For either creation is good or it is not good, and if it is good, then it cannot be good for God's goodness to be destroyed.

At the same time, I want to be careful not to underwrite mawkish sentimentality. Irwin never romanticized "wildlife," and neither should we. He never imagined that if one simply spent enough time caring for a crocodile that it would become something of a pet or a friend. That was, of course, neither his task nor his calling. His job was to help spread the good word of wildlife conservation. He never assumed that such creatures, even though he was acting on their behalf, would thank or love him for it. Yet ironically this is what makes his witness all the more interesting. His love for these creatures (he called snakes, crocs, spiders, and many other dangerous creatures "beauts") is all the more impressive as it was, often, non-reciprocal. He did not love a creature because of the possibility of a mutual love affair; rather, he loved these creatures simply because they were creatures. He loved them because they reflect the mystery of creation. For this reason, I have never questioned the sincerity of his constant labeling of them as beautiful.

Many times, as I watched the "Crocodile Hunter Diaries," I would reflect on Isaiah 11:6: "The wolf shall live with the lamb, the leopard shall lie down with the kid, the calf and the lion and the fatling together, and a little child shall lead them." When one watched the crocodile hunter in action, it was easy to get the idea that he was an example of the kind of child God calls us to be if we are to inherit God's kingdom. He never seemed to see the world that most "responsible adults" demand we embody; instead, he looked upon creation with the eyes of a child—one that could play over the "hole of the asp" and put his "hand on the adder's den" (Isa. 11:8).

Nevertheless, Steve Irwin was killed by one of the very creatures that he loved so much. The fact that a stingray plunged its spine into his chest while he was filming a documentary on the deadliest creatures in the ocean should not be lost on us. We live in a rebellious world, and no one understood this better than Irwin. Creation, all of creation, is fallen and awaits redemption. We all pine for that moment when "nothing harmful will take place on the Lord's holy mountain" (Isa. 11:9), but until then, all we have are glimpses of God's peaceable kingdom. Steve Irwin provided us with such a glimpse.

Originally published as "Crocodile Lover: Learning from Steve Irwin," *The Christian Century* 123.20, Oct. 3, 2006, pp. 9-10.

## Discussion Questions:

Steve Irwin wanted to be remembered for his "passion and enthusiasm." As Fredrick Buechner said in *Wishful Thinking*, "The place God calls you to is where your deep gladness and the world's deep hunger meet." This is really about passion, purpose, and enthusiasm. Where does your passion and enthusiasm lie? Where does your church's passion and enthusiasm lie?

Steve Irwin provided us with glimpses of God's "peaceable kingdom." What glimpses of it does this chapter provides? Where else have you glimpsed it?

In Genesis, God commands humanity to "have dominion" over creation. Dominion means something to the effect of care-giving or nurturing. We see in Mark 1:13 (in a rather obscure but very powerful verse) that Jesus was tempted and even "wild beasts" were there. God is up to something in Jesus. Our transformation is going somewhere.

Let's do a little theology: Reflect on Irwin's life, God's command, and Jesus in Mark 1:13. What is God saying to us, through this exercise, about creation?

*Chapter Four*

# A Dispossessed Carpenter's Son and a Possessed Farmer

*Faith is not belief despite evidence but a life lived in scorn of the consequences.*
—Clarence Jordan

**POPULARLY KNOWN** as the "theologian in overalls," Clarence Jordan was a man of many talents.[9] He was a farmer, a Greek scholar, and a Christian activist. He was also incredibly witty. Once while being paraded through a rather lavish church, the minister took Jordan outside to watch the sun set over the steeple. As the sun cast a magnificent spotlight on the regal cross that crowned the top of the church, the minister boasted: "That cross alone cost us ten thousand dollars." Jordan looked at the cross and then looked back at the minister and said, "You got cheated. Times were when Christians could get them for free."[10] Apparently, Jordan was not impressed.

Born on July 29, 1912, in the small town of Talbotton, Georgia, Jordan grew up in a comfortable home seasoned with devout Baptist convictions. Like all other children growing up in the South, he was raised in the center of a racially divided environment. Despite his own Protestant tradition's complicity with racist policies, ideologies, and practices, it was his ecclesial formation that led to his unease with racism. Though there were members of his own Baptist church who would sing hymns one moment and torture blacks the next, Jordan, at a very young age, understood the theological claims of the familiar children's hymn, "Jesus Loves the Little Children," with its emphasis on Jesus love for little children, all children, all colors, all precious in his sight.[11]

Jordan did not think that those around him actually believed the words of this song, for if they did they would either stop singing it or live into it. But how, in a culture systematically structured to breed racism, does one embody the subversive meaning of this hymn?

Jordan eventually found help in three particular New Testament passages: Acts 2:44, Galatians 3:27-29, and Matthew 5:12-7:27. The latter passage is the Sermon on the Mount, and it was this text—along with the entire story of Jesus and the prophetic calling of the suffering servant in the Old Testament—which convinced Jordan that discipleship required a life of nonviolence as well as a radical spirit of forgiveness. If the Son of God could be innocently executed by the very powers that he came to redeem and would, nevertheless, redeem creation through forgiveness, then it must be assumed that Christians must also enact this radical form of forgiveness. For Jordan, Christian witness entails more than the preaching of a crucified God; one must be willing to enact the story of this crucified God. Nonviolence, love of enemy and forgiveness of one's persecutor, even when the other is not seeking it, were givens for Jordan. His reading of the Sermon on the Mount demanded an acceptance of nonviolence.

The other two passages, Galatians 3:27-29 and Acts 2:44, provided specifics as to how to address the twin problems of racism and involuntary poverty. Both Martin Luther King Jr. and Malcolm X had made it painfully clear that these two problems were, by design, intertwined. Jordan understood that the church was just as guilty as the state in terms of its treatment of African-Americans. Together with the state, the church had created and maintained a network of relations that systematically oppressed black people. The church, while proving to be a resource in the fight against this oppression, was nonetheless among its chief architects. Jordan's translation of Galatians 3:27-29 was, therefore, an attempt to show the church how her life was being co-opted by the cultural evils of the times:

> You who were initiated into the Christian fellowship are Christian allies. No more is one white and another a Negro; no more is one a slave and the other a free man; no longer is one male and the other a female. For you all are as one in Christ Jesus. And if you are Christ's men, then you are the true "white men," noble heirs of a spiritual heritage.[12]

By translating Paul's letter to the Galatians as letters to the white southern churches of Georgia, Jordan was attempting to reveal the fundamentally dissident nature of Jesus' life. Jesus' disciples should not support a political order predicated on the subordination of some humans to others; rather, Jesus' disciples should be calling it into question by their very form of life. Upon baptism, there is no longer male nor female, Jew nor Greek, black nor white (nor red nor yellow). There is only one body: the body of Christ. Jordan demanded that Christians acknowledge and live into this one body. For an answer to the shape such a life might take, Jordan became a farmer.

In 1942, Jordan and his wife Florence, along with another couple, Martin and Mabel England, moved to a 440-acre plot of land near Americus, Georgia, to create an interracial Christian farming community. Despite the land being completely barren, save one seedling pecan tree, Jordan referred to it as a demonstration plot for the kingdom of God. On this desolate plot of land the Jordans would attempt to embody the call of Christian living. They called it The Koinonia Farm. The basis of *Koinonia*, which means "fellowship" or "communion," stems from Acts 2:44-47:

> All who believed were together and had all things in common; they would sell their possessions and goods and distribute the proceeds to all, as any had need. Day by day, as they spent much time together in the temple, they broke bread at home and ate their food with glad and generous hearts, praising God and having the good will of all people. And day by day the Lord added to their number those who were being saved.

Jordan surmised that if this sort of communal living was the standard practice in which the early church lived, then why not now? Had this call to live in community, to share goods, or to sell one's own possessions to provide for others, expired? How should Christians respond to this passage, and did it have anything to say to the non-racist character of God's kingdom?

Jordan wanted to give a simple answer to what he thought was a difficult question. A return to the practices of the early church, as well as the example of various monastic and Anabaptist intentional communities, was necessary if Christians were to better understand the nature of their call to be in, but not of, this world.

Their fellowship was based on four straightforward ideas: 1) treat all people with dignity; 2) respond to violence with nonviolence; 3) share all possessions; and 4) practice careful stewardship of the land loaned by God. By practicing these four tenets, Jordan hoped to not only be faithful to the witness of the New Testament but to expose how accommodating the American Christian had become toward the world. This was to be a community providing a prophetic witness against the structures of militarism, materialism, and racism.

Koinonia was quickly hated by its neighboring Christian brothers and sisters for two reasons: First, it asked that each participant become completely dispossessed. By dispossessed, I do not mean only in the sense of objects (but this was undoubtedly part of it); rather, participants were required to embody what it means to die to one's self. Fully fledged members held no private possessions, as every basic necessity was covered by a common purse. This practice alone was enough to warrant suspicion from those who suspected Koinonia to be a Communist front. Anyone who gave up possessions to share and live communally with others was assumed to be seditious.

Second, Koinonia accepted black people into the experiment. No one, argued Jordan, would be excluded from God's demonstration plot. The idea, much less the reality, that on this farm blacks worked with whites, lived with whites, worshipped with whites, and broke bread with whites was just too much for the Sumter County residents to handle. This experiment had to be put to a stop, and it would be the local God-fearing Christians who would end the madness.

By 1956, the residents of Koinonia had to routinely dodge not only bullets but explosives intended to kill them. The farm was constantly vandalized. The adults suffered persistent death threats, and even their children were not spared the harsh invective of their own school teachers who chided them in front of their classmates for being "Communists."

Though the death threats and bullets were damaging enough to the community, what almost resulted in its demise was the economic boycott leveled against the farm. Jordan could no longer buy seeds for crops or gasoline for tractors. They could no longer get insurance for their houses, farms, or farming equipment. Banks refused to do business with them, and because no one would buy, sell, or trade with them, they faced near-collapse.

Since growing crops was next to impossible, they were able to manage marketing pecans. During the next several years, they began shelling pecans and finding buyers, primarily from out of state, who were willing to buy from them. With typical Jordan wit, their slogan was, "Shipping the Nuts Out of Georgia." This kept Koinonia afloat while the threats, shootings, and boycott slowly, throughout the early 1960s, ceased.

Despite finding a new means of survival, the constant persecution of the farm took its toll. By 1963, only four adults remained living on the farm. Though many would continue to volunteer their time to this attempt to embody Jordan's vision of Christian practice, it was clear that something would have to change or the farm would perish. Today, Koinonia still sells pecans, but it is primarily famous for being the birthplace of Habitat for Humanity.

In 1968, Millard and Linda Fuller visited Koinonia and decided that what was needed was better housing for the poor of Georgia. One year after this change in direction, just before the first house was being built, Clarence Jordan died of a heart attack. Yet his vision for peace, racial reconciliation, and justice toward the poor and oppressed live on in not only Americus but throughout the world due to its association with Habit for Humanity International and The Fuller Center for Housing. The theologian in overalls, who rarely receives due recognition for his role in the civil rights movement, planted the seeds for a different kind of land. It was a demonstration of the kingdom of God, and it is still with us today.

## Discussion Questions:

York claims, "For Jordan, Christian witness entails more than the preaching of a crucified God; one must be willing to enact the story of this crucified God. Nonviolence, love of the enemy, and the forgiveness of one's persecutor, even when they are not seeking it, were 'givens' for Jordan." What are your "givens"? Where do they derive? How do they match up with Jesus?

Read Acts 2:44-47 and answer these questions:

1. How did Jordan's Koinonia Farm practice being the Acts 2 church?

2. How does the twenty-first century church do or not do this today?

3. What are ways that we can put an Acts 2 church into practice?

*Chapter Five*

# A Couple of Ineffective, Foolish Old Women

*Don't call me a saint. I don't want to be dismissed that easily.*
—Dorothy Day

**WHENEVER I AM TEMPTED** to see works of charity and obedience to Christ as ineffectual, I think of Dorothy Day and Anneken Heyndricks. Though four centuries and different denominational affiliations separate these women, it is the one thing they have in common that brings them together: their foolish display of Christ-like love.

Dorothy Day, along with Peter Maurin and other radical twentieth-century Christians, started the Catholic Worker Movement. Catholic Worker houses shelter and feed the destitute as a practice of Christian discipleship. Jesus in no uncertain terms told us that whatever we do to the least of these we do to him, so it is to those on the streets that the Catholic Worker attempts to provide care. These Christians feed the hungry and clothe the cold, and visitors understand that it is because of their faith in God that such a movement exists.

Their way of life, however, has not been without serious sacrifices. Day was jailed multiple times in her life (her last trip to jail was when she was seventy-five!) for supporting the rights of the working class. Catholic Workers live among those they are called to help, often take vows of poverty, and live lives of nonviolence. Their way of life is a small yet powerful example of taking the gospel seriously. It is what the Protestant theologian Karl Barth called "expressing gratitude toward God."

On one particularly busy morning at a Catholic Worker house, an agent of the Federal Bureau of Investigation visited Day and asked about their activities. Especially into the mid-twentieth century, the FBI, along with the CIA, was extremely interested in any groups which went to such extremes to care for the poor. Catholic Worker teaching of sharing possessions, as outlined in Acts 2:44-45, along with their refusal to participate in violence, was alarming to the FBI becauses the FBI assumed that their sharing of goods and pacifism had something to do with Communism. Clearly the authorities understood little about either Communism or Christianity! Nevertheless, the agent was sent to this particular Catholic Worker house with a mission: He wanted to know why these Christians were doing what they were doing.

In rather characteristic fashion, Day turned the conversation on the agent. She first explained that their particular way of life was an attempt to follow Jesus. She then asked him why their existence was so threatening to the U.S. government. The agent became defensive and told Day, as he cheerfully patted the pistol in his holster, that he felt in no way threatened. Day asked, with genuine bafflement, why a grown man would need protection against a bunch of "skinny children and old women." The agent quickly disappeared.

On the other end of the denominational spectrum is sixteenth-century Anneken Heyndricks. Heyndricks, whom the *Martyrs Mirror* tells us was a frail woman in her fifties who could neither read nor write, was arrested by the local church-state authorities for being an Anabaptist.

The term *Anabaptist* refers to a rebaptizing. The Anabaptists were a group of radical reformers who broke away from both the Catholics and the Protestants in the sixteenth century to protest the merger of church and state, infant baptism, and the practice of violence. (They are visible today in groups such as the Mennonites, Amish, Brethren, and Hutterites.) Many of them, baptized as infants, rejected this baptism and underwent a "believers baptism" as adults. Unfortunately, according to state law, rebaptism was a federal offense punishable by death. To paraphrase Stanley Hauerwas, the one thing Catholics and Protestants could agree on in the sixteenth century was that it was a good thing to kill the Anabaptists—and kill the Anabaptists they did.

Heyndricks understood well that her becoming an Anabaptist could mean her death. Reminiscent of the first three centuries of Christianity, believers baptism in the sixteenth century was a dangerous practice that no one embarked on lightly. Nevertheless, Heyndricks accepted the teachings of these radical reformers and was duly arrested for her worship in a non-state church.

Though she was tortured (by other "official" Christians), she neither cursed nor renounced her faith. One of the bailiffs, fed up with her obstinacy, said, "Sir Albert, our Chaplain, is such a holy fellow that the ought to be mounted in fine gold; and you will not hear him but make sport of him; hence you must die in your sins, so far are you strayed from God."[13]

They suspended Heyndricks by her hands. When even after long periods of severe torture she still did not recant, they sentenced her to be executed. She thanked the lords and asked forgiveness had she sinned against them. Such humility displeased the authorities to such a degree that, to quell her praises, they filled her mouth with gunpowder and burned her at the stake.

One thing both Day and Henydricks have in common is their insistence that what constitutes Christian living is not effectiveness but obedience. Day complained that her work appeared to do little good, and she was often overwhelmed by her inability to fill the need of all those who came to her. Heyndricks accepted the fullness of Christ in a different church and lived only long enough to suffer for it with no understanding of how her decision was effective in any calculated sense of the word. Yet, in gazing upon these two faithful women, we see that obedience has never been without effect.

As the above anecdotes suggest, simple acts of worship, such as feeding the hungry, sharing one's goods, and turning the other cheek, remain an affront to both the world and, unfortunately, many within the church. The political and social implications of practicing Christianity are apparent and often deemed intolerable. What can the world do but take notice of such lives as Dorothy Day's and Anneken Heyndricks' and respond with either bewilderment or hostility? Such lives are both foolish and a scandal to the wise.

Echoing St. Paul, William James wrote that we know the truthful ones by the lives they lead.[14] When God declares that we will be God's people, our lives must correspond to this declaration so that people recognize us as God's people. Our witness becomes our best argument for the existence of God. Our lives must be lived in such a way that if Christ were not resurrected then our lives would be unintelligible. Our concrete bodies are, therefore, the substance by which God wills to create a kingdom.

Originally published as "Holy Fools," *The Mennonite* 6.7, April 1, 2003, p. 11.

## Discussion Questions:

"Success" and "effectiveness" are the two big catchwords of the day. One does not have to look far on the bestsellers list to find books that deal with how to make an "effective" or "successful" church, business, or life. However, this might not be the call of God. Read Isaiah 6 and consider, in light of Day and Heyndricks, whether or not we should focus more on obedience rather than success and effectiveness.

Day and Heyndricks both realized what Isaiah heard: "The holy seed is its stump." What does this mean to God's people and the task we are given?

*Chapter Six*

# MANIAC OR MARTYR?

*The tyrant dies and his rule is over, the martyr dies and his rule begins.*
—Soren Kierkegaard

**CRAWLING OUT OF JENIN'S DEBRIS,** the young woman made her way southeast to Jerusalem. At the main center market at Ja'fa Road, surrounded by hundreds of Jews and Arabs, she detonated her belt bomb, killing at least seven and wounding more than eighty. Recalling the Passover martyr-massacre of the preceding week—when two celebrated young women, Palestinian Ayat al-akhras and Jewess Rachel Levy, etched their visage into the world's conscience—the world again stood numb and horrified, bewildered and intrigued before this contorted martyrdom.

Pondering this phenomenon, sociologist Daniel Boyarin, in his book *Dying for God,* identifies a genre of "holy martyrdom" which constitutes a moral core of Judaic, Christian, and perhaps even Muslim civilization. This culture of martyrdom is epitomized between the Maccabean and Bar Kochba Revolts (150 B.C.E. to 150 C.E.). Dying for God, that is, confessing and not disowning the name of God, is found in "Maccabees, gladiators, Socrates, Jesus on the cross."[15]

The central event of this *modus moriendi* is the crucifixion of Jesus. A martyr-death deemed expedient, "for the people," by Rome and Jerusalem (John 11:50), and as "necessary for salvation" (Luke 24:26) by Christians, Jesus dies "for the world" in love, forgiveness, and obedience "to the way of God." Martyrdom, godly witness to "the way," accords with Torah and Gospel (*taurut* and *injil* in Islam). It serves justice and truth and in forgiveness offers sacrifice without violence for peace. Such "dying for God" seeks to evade, not invite, martyrdom. Abrahamic faiths love life; they do not seek death. Therefore, the first task of the martyr is to flee. Martyrdom is not suicide.

On an "unholy Friday," when a twenty-year-old woman blasts herself and others to bits for the Orthodox pathologists and their tweezers, and when this grievous act follows that fateful Passover bombing just days before we must ask this: What is authentic martyrdom? Pulitzer Prize-winner Tom Friedman wrote in the *New York Times* (April 8, 2001) that, while we might honor the martyrdom of Mahatma Gandhi or Martin Luther King Jr, these other offerings were nothing but "terrorist homicides," breaching the sacred Sixth Commandment. Consider several examples of such deeds:

Mark Juergensmeyer describes the act of a self-conceived martyr—Brooklyn physician Baruch Goldstein, who

> on February 24, 1994, the night before the celebration of Purim—a holiday marking the deliverance of Jews from extinction at the hand of their oppressors (he had heard a Palestinian shout "*it bah al-yahud*: slaughter the Jews")—Dr. Baruch Goldstein went to the shrine at the Tomb of the Patriarchs in Hebron/al Kahil. The shrine is located above the Cave of Machpelah, the site where Abraham, Sarah and Isaac were said to have been entombed 3000 years ago. The Mosque of Ibrahim has stood there since the seventh century. Goldstein pulled out a Galil assault rifle he had hidden in his coat and fired into the worshiping throng of men and boys kneeling on the floor . . . he fired 111 shots, killing 30 and injuring scores more before he was overwhelmed by the crowd and pummeled to death."[16]

Less reprehensible, perhaps even acceptable, Dietrich Bonhoeffer's martyrdom is morally complex. Associated with the failed assassination attempt on Adolph Hitler's life (July 20, 1944) and at least familial conspiracy (Hans Von Dohnanyi, brother-in-law), Bonhoeffer was imprisoned for resisting the Nazi usurpation of the divine name, witnessing, with Niemoller, "*Gott ist mein fuhrer*." Pastor Bonhoeffer was executed on the Flossenberg gallows days before the liberation of Germany by the Allies.

In the mid-1960s, several Buddhist monks immolated themselves in the main street in Saigon to protest the American-South Vietnamese War against the so-called Viet Cong "freedom fighters." This witness, along with other highly visible acts (such as the My Lai Massacre) swayed world opinion and American resolve against the war.

Without weapons, and renouncing even mental violence, Gandhi not only sought to mediate and ameliorate hatred between Muslims, Hindus, and Christians in the Indian subcontinent but led the Salt March to the sea. Falling under the British clubs and guns until bodies piled up like sacrificial fire-ants, they finally prevailed in a nonviolent resistance that would inspire the American civil rights movement, Dr. King's martyrdom, and the modern commitment to peace with justice.

Dirk Willems, sixteenth-century Dutch Anabaptist and long a hero to many in Anabaptist traditions, was persecuted for practicing the Christian faith in a way offensive to both the Catholic and Protestant churches. He practiced believers baptism and nonviolence. A hired thief-catcher was in hot pursuit of Dirk as they approached a semi-frozen canal. Dirk safely crossed the canal, but the mercenary was not so fortunate. The ice gave way under the latter's weight. Yet Dirk, seeing that his pursuer was drowning, raced back to save his life. As the story is told in the *Martyrs' Mirror*, the thief-catcher desired to let him go, but the magistrate insisted on his arrest, and Dirk Willems was burned at the stake for heresy.

In these scenarios, we begin to discern a legitimate martyrdom and to distinguish such from illegitimate expressions. Our argument contends that a faithful witness to the way of God requires the kind of justice that assumes peacefulness that in turn produces an authentic martyrdom. Anything else is a madness whereby "those who live by the sword die by the sword" and intensify the cycle of violence (Matt. 26:52).

This "God way" is promulgated in the teaching of Israel's prophets. In haunting words, applicable to the U.S. and Israel, Arabia and Palestine, Jeremiah speaks to the people of the Holy Land and to all nations:

> For if you truly amend your ways and your doings, if you truly act justly one with another, if you do not oppress the alien, the orphan, and the widow, or shed innocent blood in this place, and if you do not go after other gods to your own hurt, then I will dwell with you in this place, in the land that I gave of old to your ancestors forever and ever. (Jer. 7:4-7)

Originally published as "Maniac or Martyr?" *The Mennonite* 6.16, August 19, 2003 pp. 16-17. Co-written with Kenneth Vaux.

## Discussion Questions

One thing a "faithful witness" does is reflect the character of God. How do the martyrs in this chapter reflect the character of God? What are "character traits" of God we can see in their lives?

Read Micah 6:1-8. We find that God has taken Israel to court over their "weariness." They have become weary in their worship and witness of who God is, so God takes them to court. What causes weariness in our relationship with God? What does the Lord require? How do the martyrs show what the Lord requires?

# PART II

# Our Politics

## Introduction: Lions and Lambs

*But our citizenship [commonwealth] is in heaven, and it is from there we are expecting a Savior, the Lord Jesus Christ.*
—Phillipians 3:20

**THE CHRISTIAN ETHICIST** Stanley Hauerwas and the Methodist Bishop William Willimon argue in their book *Resident Aliens* that Christianity does not *have* a politic; rather, Christianity *is* a politic.[17] By claiming that Christianity is a politic, they are arguing against the tendency of Christians to adopt whatever political theory they find to be most congruent with their understanding of the gospel. This is ill-advised, however, because there is no political theory that fits the gospel; rather, the gospel reveals an alternative way of life to political theories.

Christians do not adopt our understanding of what it means to be political from the world, nor do we simply assume that the political ideologies of the world are somehow superior to how we organize ourselves. I fear that when we assume we must adopt democratic, socialistic, or even anarchistic principles to supplement or constitute ourselves, then we end up privileging the world's understanding of itself. The argument within these pages is that Christianity stems from a different understanding, a different sociology so to speak, because it is a commonwealth constituted by the broken yet resurrected body of Christ. This makes for an "upside-down" politic that cannot help but lead to conclusions contrary to prevailing accounts of wisdom.

This next section attempts to deal with what it means to embody the gospel's upside-down politic under the religious rubric established by the United States. This does not mean that the first section, which dealt more with particular people embodying their convictions, was not an exercise in politics. I hesitate to even divide these sections, as it is not clear to me how any of the following chapters are any more political than the previous ones. Nevertheless, the following do share a common motif as they attempt to challenge Christianity's complicity with the empire's understanding of what it means to be political.

I begin with a conversation held in one of my classes as to what the just Christian response to Saddam Hussein should have been. The argument here is not merely against the death penalty (truly an odd thing for Christians to support, given what happened to Jesus, Peter, Paul, and many others within the first 300 years of Christianity); it is an argument for Christians to take seriously their mission to spread the gospel. That is what remains at the heart of each of these chapters. What does evangelism have to do with the understanding of justice after Jesus? This question is asked throughout each chapter as I discuss nuns getting arrested, the sacred nature of voting, and how the unknown saints keep the world turning.

*Chapter Seven*

# Death by Hanging Is Way Too Easy! (Try Torture Instead)

*If we believe that murder is wrong and not admissible in our society, then it has to be wrong for everyone, not just individuals but governments as well.*
—Helen Prejean

*Three things belong to God and do not belong to men: the irrevocable, the irreparable and the indissoluble. Woe to men if they introduce it in their laws!*
—Victor Hugo

**BEFORE SADDAM HUSSEIN** was hanged, a student in one of my religious studies classes asked how I thought Christians should respond to Saddam Hussein's death sentence. I said, "That's way too easy! Torture is what he deserves!" Some students smiled happily while others, thankfully, found my answer to be problematic. Before I could finish my response, many students (well, a few at least) quickly suggested that capital punishment was wicked enough, but how could one suggest torture? So I immediately sent them down a less direct road, and asked them to give me a definition of justice.

Replies varied, but we finally agreed that, at least within the body politic of our culture, the Latin account of justice, which is *suum cuique*—"to each what is due"—was adequate in terms of fairness and, in terms of punishment or retributive justice, people should get what they deserve (though this definition may or may not contain problems, let the reader be aware that this was an *introductory* course in religion).

Of course, attempting to discern what each person is due or "deserves" tends to beg a lot of questions: What is due to Native Americans for being all but annihilated in the name of manifest destiny? What is due to African Americans for building our wealthy nation for free? What is due to women for centuries upon centuries of patriarchal oppression? Plus, *who* gets to decide what is due to these groups, and how do we (whoever this "we" is) negotiate what the culprits of such injustices deserve? I am guessing that what a Native American, African American, or a woman thinks is justice will differ from not just one another but from the power of a white, male-dominated culture that made such injustice possible.

It seems that appeals to justice are always rooted in particularity, and it is very difficult to assume some sort of monolithic account of justice that will suffice for all people. For whoever is privileged enough to decide what constitutes justice, the giving and receiving of what one deserves or is due to another, will offer an account that favors a way of seeing the world at odds with various other people's comprehension of justice. So how is one to respond to injustice in light of relativized justice?

These problems aside, the class wanted to know what this had to do with the sentencing of Hussein. (They were, unsurprisingly, not interested in issues of distributive justice for the crimes committed by our ancestors or by us in the present.) Do we just concede that there is no universal account of justice and let him go unpunished? I attempted to divert the question back on the class by asking them what they thought we deserved as a people whose way of life had been made possible by the genocide and subjugation of various people of differing racial, ethnic, and gendered bodies.

Silence was the primary response. So I attempted to convince them that, as Christians, we should first note that justice defined as what one deserves fails. We must first ask the theological question: What do Christians deserve? The answer is, and has always been throughout the history of Christianity, death. God created the world good, but we are "evil from youth" and rebel against the Creator (Gen. 8:21). Nevertheless, God is good, just, loving, and holy, and, therefore, responds to us with an account of justice that does not give us what we deserve but undoes the entire logic of both retributive and distributive justice. God's love is not predicated on either punishment or fairness but on perpetual gratuitous charity. God sends God's only Son to save us (this is God's justice), and we respond by killing him. Nevertheless, because God's justice is also God's charity (justice and charity do not occupy separate spheres within God—God's justice *is* God's charity), God exercises patience with us and grants us far more than what is due to us or what we deserve. Christians, therefore, are called to imitate the character of God and to embody this kind of justice that is charitable justice.

We do not simply think about what is due someone, though at the bare minimum we must think this through (that in and of itself would be enough to turn the world upside down); rather, we must attempt to think about the injustices we have committed and continue to commit and of how to repent of these while responding to those we have wronged in ways that reveal we are redeemed.

In terms of fairness and doing penance for crimes we commit, we humble ourselves to the victims of the crime and ask their help in showing us how to make amends. In terms of punishing those who commit crimes against us, we subvert this world's understanding of justice by going beyond it—by *not* giving what others deserve. Rather, we reflect the very grace and forgiveness that God bestows upon us in order that the world may know God.

Back to the case of Saddam Hussein. In class I said that death was too easy. I said that it was too easy because, in the first place, it would make him a martyr in the eyes of his followers, and, second, it let us off the hook of doing what God demands of us. I concluded, therefore, that Hussein should be tortured.

However, the class did not allow me to finish my sentence on *how* he should be tortured. I told them that as Christians we never assume that anyone is outside the transforming love of God and that we not only live by the hope that someone like Hussein could undergo a radical conversion (and aren't all conversions radical?), but that we must attempt to show God's love to such persons so they have the opportunity to convert.

So I suggested that the proper response to Saddam was to become missionaries and have one of us go every day to his prison and witness to him. To be honest, I can't think of anything that would have been like to torture him more than a bunch of Christians attempting to convert him, but, then again . . . wouldn't he have deserved it?

Originally published as "Death By Hanging is Way Too Easy," *Christian Ethics Today* issue 63, no. 1, 2007, pp. 24-25.

## Discussion Questions

Given that Jesus died on a cross, forgiving his killers, how should Christians reevaluate how they understand *justice*?

How does Jesus' command to love one's enemies come into effect in the case of known terrorists?

Is any person beyond the saving grace of God? Does capital punishment assume some people are beyond God's salvation?

In terms of persecutors of Christians, there were few worse than Paul of Tarsus. Yet, he ended up writing a third of the New Testament. If he were in the twenty-first century, many Christians would demand his death due to the blood on his hands. Should this not challenge how Christians understand the death penalty? Since both Jesus and Paul suffered the death penalty, how does this affect how we think about those we have in our power to put to death?

*Chapter Eight*

# FROM AFGHANISTAN TO GEORGIA

*If . . . the machine of government . . . is of such a nature that it requires you to be the agent of injustice to another, then, I say, break the law.*
—Henry David Thoreau

**DOROTHY AND GWEN HENNESSEY**, sisters both biologically and as members of Dubuque's Sisters of St. Francis, received the *Pacem in Terris* Peace and Freedom Award in 2002. The Roman Catholic nuns share company with a distinguished list of other recipients: Mother Teresa, Dr. Martin Luther King Jr., Sister Helen Prejean, Cesar Chavez, Dorothy Day, and many others.

The Hennessey sisters also happen to be recent convicts. After being banned from the Western Hemisphere Institute for Security Cooperation (originally named the School of Americas), the sisters violated the ban by joining in with more than 5,000 other demonstrators advocating for the school's closure. Following a six-month prison sentence, the sisters were released and honored with the award that commemorates Pope John XXIII's 1963 encyclical letter, *Pacem in Terris.* It is in this letter that Pope John invites all people—regardless of particular faith or nationality—to strive for peace. The sisters' insistence on ending those things that perpetuate violence was what led them both to prison and this award. Precisely such service to what the sisters' claim is simply "faithfulness to Christ" is what truly renders them, in the words of Aristotle, "political animals."

For those who do not know what the WHISC is, a little history lesson—along with a brief list of the kind of graduates it has produced—may be illuminating. The U.S. Army School of Americas (SOA), as it was dubbed in 1946, was founded in Panama as an effort to promote friendly relations between the U.S. military and its Central and South American counterparts. In 1984, the school moved to Fort Benning, Georgia, where it has continued to train Latin American soldiers in counter-resistance to drug trafficking and insurrection.

After the Pentagon was forced to release training manuals used at the school (revealing the encouragement of torture, extortion, and execution), Congress authorized the WHISC to replace the SOA and, in 2001, the name was changed. Its critics, however, have viewed this change as an attempt to diffuse public protest. It remains apparent that, though the name has changed, the tactics remain the same.

It is often said that one can know teachers by the kind of students they produce. This school reflects this aphorism well. Graduates of WHISC are responsible for some of the more notorious human rights abuses in Latin America. Among the WHISC's infamous alumni are dictators Manuel Noriega and Omar Torrijos of Panama, Guillermo Rodriguez of Ecuador, Leopoldo Galtieri and Roberto Viola of Argentina, Hugo Banzer Suarez of Bolivia, and Juan Velasco Alvarado of Peru.

Some of the more mediocre students have not faired quite as well. Their list of atrocities include (but are in no way limited to) the assassination of Archbishop Oscar Romero; the slaughtering of nearly 1,000 civilians in the El Mozote Massacre; the killing of more than 3,000 people during Augusto Pinochet's seventeen-year reign in Chile; and the torture of Carlos Mauricio—a science teacher at Balboa High School in San Francisco who, paradoxically, fled to the U.S. in the early 1980s to escape soldiers trained by the U.S.!

It is true that, due to public protests, the school revised its curriculum in 1989 to integrate training on human rights. Many people feel that this is hardly enough. Respect for human dignity barely stands a chance when one is taught how to torture and kill fellow human beings. Which brings us to the bottom line: WHISC operates as a school that trains its students how to deal with its enemies in a very particular manner—by any means necessary. This kind of formation is not only directly at odds with the Christian narrative, but it also trains people how to locate enemies that are not even deserving of such a title. How is it that Christians in America can—in good conscience—support this school when it trains soldiers how to kill fellow Christians (like Romero) in other countries? The question is one of allegiance: Does baptism link us to all Christians regardless of nationality? Or, does patriotic fervor blind us to our own disobedience to Christ?

This brings me back to our good sisters. Their witness reminds us that following Jesus is hardly an apolitical affair. True political behavior is accompanying with a bodily imitation of Christ. An imitation that, as it placed Jesus in the center of political controversy (his kingdom is, after all, a rival kingdom), places his followers in the position of narrating the world in such a way that may lead them to the same place it led him: the cross.

What have we learned from not only these two witnesses but also from a church that recognizes them as witnesses? What does this demand that we, as Christians, must say to the U.S. government? Perhaps we can say that if it can destroy terrorist training facilities in Afghanistan, it could do the same in Georgia.

Originally published in *Christian Ethics Today*, issue 46, vol. 9, no. 4, October 2003, pp. 13-14.

## Discussion Questions

Are training facilities like Ft. Benning necessary? What are they needed for? Most importantly, how does the person of Jesus redefine how we think about military bases such as this one in Georgia?

Does "patriotic fervor" for our nation-state blind us? If so, how does it shape how we view the gospel?

Ultimately, with whom do we side in this situation: Our sisters in Christ arrested for protesting this training facility, or those who would arrest them? Why? In which group might you find yourself most comfortable?

*Chapter Nine*

# On Asking Too Much

*Dan and I went to prison because we believed that Christianity and revolution are synonymous. Jesus Christ was a nonviolent revolutionary; therefore, Christians have a duty to subvert society to create a world where justice prevails, particularly for the poor who must be treated with fairness and love.*
—Philip Berrigan

**THE ABOVE QUOTE** comes from Philip Berrigan's autobiography *Fighting the Lamb's War: Skirmishes with the American Empire.* On May 17, 1968, Phillip, the first Catholic priest in North America to have ever been arrested for civil disobedience, and his brother Dan (also a Catholic priest), along with seven others, walked into the draft board in Catonsville, Maryland, and burned draft files. After that, they said prayers, submitted themselves to the government, and were eventually sentenced to time in a federal prison.

Rather than spend their lives just writing and talking about theology, they decided to perform it. In an attempt to expose to North American Christians the idolatry often demanded of governments, especially in times of war, the Berrigan brothers chose to burn draft files with homemade napalm to symbolically show what was being used on both combatants and civilians in Vietnam. The government's response confirmed their suspicions: for burning paper, you serve time in jail; for burning humans, you're a national hero.

This next story is slightly different, but I hope we can locate the connections. In the third chapter of the book of Daniel, we find the story of King Nebuchadnezzar's vain attempt to have all of those under his command worship his gods.[18] The king, who only moments earlier had proclaimed his undying loyalty to the God of Israel, created a massive and magnificent golden statue and commanded all people of various nations and languages, at the cue of his "entire musical ensemble," to fall down and worship. As the music played, we are told, "all the peoples, nations, and languages fell down and worshiped" the golden statue (Dan. 3:7).

This is not entirely true. A few refused to bow to such obvious idolatry. Scripture says that there were "certain Jews" who had been "appointed over the affairs of the province of Babylon" that had refused the orders of the king. Their names were Shadrach, Meshach, and Abednego, and their disobedience was quickly reported.

Unsurprisingly, this enraged Nebuchadnezzar. He sent for the three and commanded them to fall down and worship his creation. If they persisted in their noncompliance they would be cast into a furnace to be consumed by fire.

Our heroes did not relent. They told the king they felt no need to defend their actions; furthermore, if their God wanted to save them from the furnace, then God would. "But if not," they continued, "be it known to you, O King, that we will not serve your gods and we will not worship the golden statue you have set up" (Dan. 3:18).

The story ends, as many of us are aware, with the three surviving the fire and the king going mad. What is most unnerving about this tale now is the manner in which it has been so easily domesticated and romanticized for the kind of disembodied Christianity prevalent in North America. The first time I heard this story, for instance, I could not have been much older than six, and yet it was told to me in such a way that I never got the idea that the actions of Shadrach, Meshach, and Abednego were either remotely radical or political. Of course, it may be a bit much to assume that at six years of age I should know anything more than the story itself, but following a few decades of immersion in the church I would have hoped to be weaned from milk and fed solid food (1 Cor. 3:2).

Rare is the occasion that one hears this story told in such a way that we might find *ourselves* threatened by something analogous to a furnace (at least a jail cell). Perhaps even more telling is how, despite the fact that these three men were well aware that God might not save them, they still refused to accommodate the king's wishes. Interestingly, they all actually served the king. Yet they were still capable of discerning when a leader had asked that which cannot be given. I just wonder how this story could be told so that we too could discern when what is demanded of us becomes an occasion for idolatry.

Perhaps this story is too easy. The idolatry is plain to see, even by a six-year-old child. What may be required, therefore, is a bit of that solid food intended for the mature in body and spirit (Heb. 5:14). What resources are necessary for Christians today to understand when something is being asked of us that should not, nor must not, be given to those who call themselves our benefactors?

We do have the resources necessary to make such careful distinctions via Scripture and tradition. I say Scripture and tradition because Scripture is not self-interpreting. Scripture is easily manipulated to suit our own purposes, therefore we rely on tradition, as well as a community of faith—an actual body of believers—to help us interpret Scripture well and to hold us accountable when we fail to do so.

Yet part of what the Nebuchadnezzar anecdote teaches us is that our best sources are biographical. The stories of Daniel, Shadrach, Meshach, and Abednego; Ruth, Esther and Sarah; Hosea, Amos, and Jeremiah; John, Peter, Paul, and Mary all constitute a tradition of interpretation still exemplified in the lives of those who continue to conform their will to God.

This is why the Catholic Church has saints. Saints are those the church, as a body politic, has agreed help us to understand Scripture by their very lives. Protestants and Anabaptists may use the word *saint* a bit differently, but we still look to those who have followed Jesus well as exemplars of what it means to have one's will conformed to God.

Though we may not agree with all of the actions performed by those rebel priests the Berrigans, is it not possible to see how, for example, their lives are made more intelligible through the aforementioned story from Daniel (or vice-versa)? If so, what does this mean for how we understand Jesus and how, in turn, we live Christ-like lives? What does it mean to follow the path of Jesus when our respective governments demand total allegiance? When Jesus demands that we love our enemies and our leaders demand that we kill them, whom do we obey? Caesar or Christ? Do we really understand the political statement that Jesus is Lord? If so, why is it not more obvious that all of the presidents we will ever have ask more of us than what is owed to them?

Unfortunately, the church is so often co-opted by the project of the state that we are no longer capable of offering a prophetic witness to the peaceable kingdom. Therefore we render it difficult for Christians to realize that our loyalties are being stretched thin.

Jesus said that we cannot serve two masters. This is exactly why it is so important for the state to dupe the church into thinking that they are both on the same trajectory. So, in a time like this, when it is apparent that whoever is in charge of the White House is going to demand more than what is owed its occupants (our bodies in service to the exact opposite of how Jesus calls us to treat our enemies), we must ask at least this one basic question: How are Christians living in a post-Christian climate, though still residing in a nominally Christian environment, going to be capable of discerning when it is time to say, "But if not [even if God does not intervene to save us], be it known to you, O King, that we will not serve your gods . . .?"

Originally published in *Christian Ethics Today issue* 67, vol. 13, no. 5, November 2007.

## Discussion Questions

Read Daniel 3:19-25. What happens when the three are thrown into the fire? What does the king see? What does he say? How does this speak to Christians, in any part of the world attempting to discern when their "kings" have asked too much from them?

What are the theological similarities and differences between the Berrigan brothers and Shadrach, Meshach, and Abednego?

The "four, walking, abound in the fire" is a great symbol of faith. What is it? What is this great "thing" that the saints and the followers of Christ share? You may want to examine John 8:27-32 for greater insight.

*Chapter Ten*

# Who Mourns the Gods? Part 1

*A god cannot survive as a memory.*
—Apollo

**THE TITLE OF THIS ARTICLE** is a swipe from the "Star Trek" (original series) episode *Who Mourns Adonais?* The crew of the Starship Enterprise find themselves captured by a powerful force of energy that has taken the shape of a human hand. While their ship remains held firmly in place, Captain Kirk and a small number of his crew make their way to the planet they were orbiting when captured.

What they find is rather shocking: a being claiming to be the Greek god Apollo. This "Apollo" alleges that humans outgrew the need for the Greek gods, necessitating the decision of the other gods (Zeus, Athena, Artemis, etc.) to choose to vanish into the cosmos, never to be heard from again. It seems that in order for gods to be gods they require subjects willing to claim them as gods—at least for the Olympians. Apollo, however, decides to wait it out. He locates a distant "Class M" planet (a planet, according to Star Trek mythology, that can host carbon-based life) and patiently awaits humanity's arrival.

After 5,000 years, humans show up only to find what kick-started much of Western civilization in the first place: a Greek god. While admitting that the worship of Greek gods and its mythology gave rise to important advances in human history, Captain Kirk declares that humanity's days of bending knees to gods, or alien races claiming to be gods, are over.

A battle, of course, ensues. Kirk, Spock, and the others outwit Apollo who, defeated, fades into the cosmos realizing that there no longer is a place for "his kind." As he dissipates he says that he only wanted to love his children and take care of them. Kirk hints at the nobility of such a claim, saying, "Would it have hurt us, to gather just a few laurel leaves?" Nevertheless, the episode ends with humanity's (and a Vulcan's) integrity remaining intact as they valiantly refuse the offer of peace and security if it requires their subordination to a higher being.

There is much to deal with in this very clever episode. The notion of gods being dependent on us for existence, the idea that security is not worth the loss of independence, as well as suggestions that religion is really just a natural phenomenon no longer necessary in the evolutionary progression of human life—all are worthy of consideration.

What I want to think about, however, are the reasons Apollo is rejected as a deity (other than Bones' technology suggesting he is a "simple humanoid"). It is important to point out that this episode, while expressing incredulity toward religious belief, is not simply an apology for atheism. Kirk suggests that one reason for his refusal to bow to Apollo is that "one god is quite adequate." Yet the viewer gets the feeling that this line was merely included as a means of avoiding outrage from, at the time, a very religiously conservative audience.

For instance, many of the Star Trek crews' reasons for refusing to worship Apollo stem from similar protests against the God of Christianity. Apollo is referred to as benevolent one moment and destructive the next. One does not have to look deep into Scripture to discover origins of such an idea. The God of Christianity is angry but for "a moment" (and what is a moment for God who is outside and beyond time?); that moment, however, means "everlasting disgrace," or complete destruction, for God's enemies (Ps. 30:5, 78:66; Gen. 19). Apollo demands complete obedience and, in return, grants his children peace; yet if they disobey, they will suffer severe punishment. Apollo's comment that "you will learn discipline" appears as mere child's play in relation to God's justice:

> [I]f you will not obey me, and do not observe all these commandments, if you spurn my statutes, and abhor my ordinances, so that you will not observe all my commandments, and you break my covenant, I in turn will do this to you: I will bring terror on you; consumption and fever that waste the eyes and cause life to pine away. You shall sow your seed in vain, for your enemies shall eat it. I will set my face against you, and you shall be struck down by your enemies; your foes shall rule over you, and you shall flee though no one pursues you. And if despite this you will not obey me, I will continue to punish you sevenfold for your sins. (Lev. 26:14-18)

I imagine Capt. Kirk would have responded to the God of Israel with as much pride and bravado as he offered Apollo.[19] Would we have still admired his prideful refusal to place himself below another?

Are we too prideful for the gods (or God)? Though North America remains an incredibly religious culture, we maintain a piety that, I believe, primarily serves us. We are so thoroughly religious, it seems, because of how we feel served by such religiosity. There is no shortage of books topping the bestseller's list that teach us how to have our Jesus and "health and wealth" too. This should cause us to pause. We are religious, I fear, because we are self-interested. There is, of course, nothing innovative about such a concern. This has been a staple argument of atheists ranging from Ludwig Feuerbach to Karl Marx, and from Friedrich Nietzsche to Sam Harris. Unfortunately, they may be right.

As North American Christians, we no longer need nor care for the God whose holiness requires a costly sacrifice. The demands of this "ancient" deity are far too high. The God of Scripture is far too threatening to our sense of self that is predicated on language such as autonomy and freedom. In turn, we have shaped this god into our own image to service our own needs. We now have a god who, as it says on our most sacred paper (money), "favors our undertakings" (*annuit copetis*).[20] We love the god whose enemies just happen to be our own. We worship the god that grants us wealth, security, and a common sense of privilege unknown throughout most of the world.

We have created a tribal deity. One that is oh-so-much like us because, as Ludwig Feuerbach astutely suggests, we are not created in the image of God as much as we create god(s) in our own image.[21] Yet we are in a dangerous predicament because we retain the language of the very God who would call such religious devotion to this deity idolatry. God is not a god. God is not another entity in the universe influenced or moved by our actions. God is not subjected to our makings of God and, therefore, cannot be reshaped and molded into our vision of who God is.

In terms of the Starship Enterprise's problem with subservience and their attendant championing of the self-made human, God is not interested in our freedom from servitude but only in our lives sacrificed to ourselves. Whether or not there are any purposeful similarities between the portrayal of Apollo on Star Trek and what the writers of Star Trek imagined to be the God of Judaism and Christianity is a question I will leave for others. What I wonder is this: Are there similarities between the Enterprise's rejection of Apollo and our fervent belief in the tribal god of the United States?

## Discussion Questions

How have we shaped God in our own image? What do you think causes us to shape God in our own image? How can we know when this has happened?

In his book *The Cost of Discipleship*, Dietrich Bonhoeffer claims that the grace of God is not cheap and that it comes with a cost. That cost is our allegiance and faithfulness to the kingdom of God. At this point, we may well be on board with Bonhoeffer. Unfortunately, however, he lowers the boom when he writes that the call of Christ bids a person to "come and die."[22] This is in line with the New Testament—yet is this not the opposite of how we in North America envision the good that discipleship entails? Have we not spiritualized this death?

What do Bonhoeffer's comments, along with York's arguments in this chapter, have to say to the "health and wealth" theologies that flood our congregations?

*Chapter Eleven*

# A Potential Non-Voting Manifesto

*The revolution will be drowned in the ballot boxes—which is not surprising, since they were made for that purpose.*
—Jean-Paul Sartre

**THERE ARE FEW THINGS** imagined more dutiful in this life than the so called "responsibility" of every North American to vote. Despite the fact that many decide, for whatever reasons, not to vote, the very idea that voting is an indispensable requirement that falls on each individual goes largely unquestioned.

Let me state at the outset that any qualms I may have about voting stem from neither apathy nor indifference. It simply makes little sense to me, given that we are, as Aristotle claimed, political animals, that anyone would or should be indifferent to voting. Christians, whom I am here addressing, should be concerned with the goods that constitute the temporal cities of this time between times, and voting is but one means of attempting to seek those goods.

Nevertheless, I often wonder if what has been passed down to us as an unquestioned duty is the only way, or even the primary way, to be political. To be more specific, is it possible for a conscientious abstention from voting to be understood as an act of politics concerned with the good of the polis? Could it function as a witness to a different order, one not predicated on the enforcement of legislation, laws, and the lording of power over one another? If so, what would be the rationale for such an objection, or at least a hesitation, to the act of voting? What sort of of witness would this attempt to make?

To answer these questions I have jotted down a few points in a modest attempt to put forth reasons why voting might be problematic for Christians. If nothing else, at least dealing with these possible objections could make us more conscientious voters—if that is what we decide part of Christian witnessing entails.

Romans 13 demands subordination to the government. Which government? All governments. Paul demanded Christian submission to powers that be because, despite how fallen they are, they are ordained by God. Rebellion against such powers is understood as rebellion against God and thus not permitted. It makes no sense, therefore, to perpetuate any order founded on explicit disobedience of Scripture. The United States of America only came into being through rebellion against the God-ordained powers of English monarchy. (The irony of this is rich as the most patriotic of souls love to use this text to demand obedience to every whim of their beloved nation-state without recognizing the hypocrisy that made it possible for it to come into being in the first place.) To vote for the maintenance of such an order seems to entail approval of disobedience against God, or at least renders Paul's command nonsensical as it can be disobeyed if enough time has elapsed from the inception of said rebellion/revolution.

Jesus requires that his disciples not be like those Gentiles who lord their power over others, even if it is for some sort of "good" (Matt. 20:25). Christians are, as he says in verse 26, not to be this way; rather, they are to be slaves to and of one another. It might be one thing if elected officials of this nation were forced to take office; instead, these are individuals who desperately want to be in power and beg and plead with the common folk for their votes, all to the tune of countless millions of dollars—spent to convince us that we should exalt those who would be like those Gentiles who lord their power over others. If we are forbidden to be like them, why would it be permissible to place them in the kind of posture Jesus decries?

Capitalism, the socio-economic order that underwrites this culture, is predicated on the seven deadly sins (lust, gluttony, greed, sloth, wrath, envy, pride). Without just one of these sins, capitalism would fold and collapse on itself. For instance, if there was no greed this economy would be destroyed. We are taught to never be satisfied, to never have our fill, to never be satiated, to remain in a perpetual state of want, all in the name of the common good. How is this even remotely akin to the kind of desires that should be produced by ecclesial formation? Goods are only good if they are shared goods, at least according to Scripture and early Christian history. Sharing goods in this culture would be a sin.

An aside, but pertinent: Let it not be lost on us that immediately after September 11, 2001, the president of the United States demanded that we the people respond neither with prayer nor patience but by . . . shopping. The interesting thing is, this was actually a morally legitimate command—as it would have been for any president, for that matter. Had people ceased spending money, the economy would have collapsed. Therefore, in such a culture one responds to terrorism via trips to the mall (along with many missiles and the country's young people). This is our way of life? This is what Christians are willing to both die and kill for? How can we vote for any potential Caesar under this sort of politic?

While we are on the subject of the seven deadly sins, let's look at one more: pride. *Pride* is a term that falls again and again from the lips of U.S. leaders. Both Scripture and tradition remind us that pride is purely representative of the fall of humankind. Because of this, there is nothing to be proud of except, inasmuch as one can boast with St. Paul, hope in Jesus. Pride has become the very means whereby we Christians are co-opted into our culture. Pride has robbed us of the resources to practice repentance, confession, humility, and servanthood—all of which are at the heart of Christianity. Voting is, de facto, an exercise in pride (especially if you find yourself on the winning side).

In the gospel of Luke, Satan takes Jesus up to the mountain top and offers him all of the kingdoms of the world:

> The devil led him up to a high place and showed him in an instant all the kingdoms of the world. And he said to him, "I will give you all their authority and splendor, for it has been given to me, and I can give it to anyone I want to. So if you worship me, it will all be yours." Jesus answered, "It is written: 'Worship the Lord your God and serve him only." (Luke 4:5-8)

Though the powers may be ordained by God, they are (as with all of creation) in rebellion against God, and according to this passage it is Satan leading this rebellion. Satan offers the kingdoms to Jesus because they belong to Satan. Satan gives them, or at least offers them, to whomever Satan pleases. All Jesus has to do, to rule the world the way most of us imagine how we are to rule it, is to worship Satan. Thus it appears that all of the kingdoms of the world, though rightly ordained for the maintenance of social harmony, are currently satanic. All you have to do to lead them is worship Beelzebub; hence my reluctance to vote for this sort of person.

Even the U.S. Constitution tempts us toward idolatry. Though written by humans (right after the rebellion against the God-ordained powers nonetheless) to protect the interests of a few wealthy white men, we are taught to understand all of life in this socio-politic through its lens. It becomes the all-encompassing hermeneutical device that enables us to determine what constitutes a good life. This is a life that leads us into hyper-atomization, self-interest, and ownership of private goods (even as it deprives others of the basic necessities of life). Through the Constitution private interests are served and protected against any claims of common ownership of God's good earth. We are to imagine that this is a good thing.

Ezekiel 16:49 says, "Behold, this was the guilt of your sister Sodom: she and her daughters had arrogance, abundant food and careless ease, but she did not help the poor and needy." Our economic order requires all of us to practice the sin of sodomy. Class-led consumer capitalism simply cannot thrive without an impoverished class. Indeed, the very basis of Adam Smith's *The Wealth of the Nations*, the quintessential text that underwrites our order, is the promise that we can all be rich (the very state Jesus seems to think a huge impediment to our salvation).

Regardless of which leaders win, they will demand my unadulterated allegiance. That is, of course, a problem in and of itself, as Christians are called to serve only one master. How this, arguably, affects Christians the most is that leaders of empires simply cannot enact the radical kind of peace Christians are to offer their enemies. Rulers, history has shown, must take up arms against their enemies. They must engage in warring, or at least threats of warring, to secure certain goods.

This is a far cry from that which Jesus calls his disciples. Jesus demands that those who would follow his lead must turn the other cheek and pray for those who persecute us. (Ever heard a president pray for enemies—except that they be destroyed?) Jesus' followers must refuse to inflict vengeance, as that belongs to God. Yet all nation-states demand the exact opposite. To be socially relevant and responsible is to forego the literal imitation of Jesus. I argue that any order that demands that a Christian not imitate Jesus is a demonic one indeed, a stumbling block for God's children.

Someone once said that the United States may be the greatest Babylon on the planet, but she is still a Babylon. As William Stringfellow astutely pointed out, if we are to read all nations biblically then we must recognize that they are all Babylons.[23] None are the Heavenly Jerusalem; if they were, then they would be the City of God. They are, therefore, parasitic on the good that is the heavenly city, and the church, as the image of this city on earth, is called to show the state that it is not the heavenly city.

That, I think, is the church's task. It is not to buttress the powers that be but to show them, through the church's witness, that whatever the powers that be are, they are not the church. One way to resist being co-opted by the powers that be, I imagine, is by neither voting nor taking office.

Voting is saying that you want these persons to enact your will, legislate it, and force it on others. Then inasmuch as these persons do this, you will support them. That is, you demand that they do what you want them to do for the betterment of how you envision the world (even as rather than seeking the peace of the city, as Jeremiah demands, this often results in attempting to *secure* the peace).

Voting and the system it entails spares Christians the burden of actually having to be the church, because now we can have the state require of others all that we think it should. We don't need to work on creating alternative communities, we don't need to be prophetic to the powers that be through the act of radical discipleship because we have become the very powers and principalities Paul claims Jesus has defeated.

By the simple refusal to vote, perhaps we can at least better see how such a power has seduced us to compromise and domesticate our faith in the name of something other than the Triune God.

These simple musings are but a few reasons I am currently hesitant to cast my vote for yet another Caesar.

Originally published as "A Non-Voting Manifesto?" *Christian Ethics Today*, issue 70, vol. 14, no. 3, Summer 2008.

## Discussion Questions

Why does voting strike such a nerve in many of us? What is it about voting that seems so sacred?

Does it matter that some people, specifically minorities and women, sacrificed much to gain the right to vote?

Briefly discuss "objections" listed in this article. What do you say about each? Which ones struck a nerve? Which ones made sense—or did not? Which can we, as Christians, put into practice?

On a dry-erase board or paper, draw a column for the kingdom of God and a column for the world's kingdoms (at least the U.S.). List words that describe each kingdom. Compare the two. What are the significant differences, and why do they matter in terms of how we live in our earthly kingdoms?

How can the decision not to vote be a political witness?

*Chapter Twelve*

# A Plea for a Few Good Christians to Move (Or, Stay Put!)

**IN ONE OF MY RELIGION CLASSES** we were reading the story of the destruction of Sodom and Gomorrah. Students wondered why God decided these two cities deserved God's wrath. After providing the standard account as delineated by various Old Testament scholars (ranging from lack of hospitality to sexual degradation), one of my students said, "Well, if God doesn't destroy Las Vegas, God is going to have to apologize to Sodom and Gomorrah."

This was not the first time I had heard such a comment, yet for some reason it sent me down a different path of thinking. After first establishing a theological argument against what it would mean for God to have to apologize for anything, I asked the student why he thought God would find it necessary to issue this rather late-coming apology. He simply stated that Las Vegas is a city predicated on and perpetuated by the sins of greed, lust, gluttony, and pride. That is, it is a place that freely, and without reservation, prides itself on indulging in the very things Christians are called to resist.

Given that I have never been there, I will have to take his

word for it (for some reason he admitted to having visited this city of sin on more than one occasion), but I have paid special attention to the commercials suggesting that "Whatever happens in Vegas stays in Vegas." I think it is probably safe to say that whatever that means, it is probably not an invitation to practice Christian virtues. I offered what I assumed to be a biblical response: "Perhaps," I said, "there are some righteous people in Las Vegas." The class immediately asked what this had to do with its righteousness, which required us to take a closer look at the story of Sodom and Gomorrah.

I told them that what I found to be most interesting about this story is, at the risk of being anachronistic, the rather humanistic approach taken by Abraham. It appears that Abraham worries about the destruction of Sodom and Gomorrah because he fears that God will destroy the righteous along with the wicked: "Far be it from you Oh Lord to do such a thing." This prompts Abraham to negotiate with God over the very act of destruction itself. Indeed, God anticipates this when God thinks about keeping it from Abraham (Gen.18:17) yet decides to let Abraham in on God's plans.

Abraham immediately protests and attempts to convince God that this would not be a good and just thing for a good and just God to do. So Abraham asks God that if there happens to be fifty righteous people within the two cities would God not spare them all? God responds with a yes. Abraham, however, is no fool. He knows it is highly unlikely there are fifty righteous people in those cities, so he proceeds to bargaining. To play it safe, he reduces the number by five. God agrees: "If there are forty-five righteous people there I will forgive the whole city."

Abraham thinks this still may not cover it so asks for five fewer, to which again God agrees. Then Abraham grows a little more brazen and asks if God would destroy such a place if there happened to be thirty righteous people. Again God agrees to withhold punishment. Abraham continues. He pushes the number down to twenty, even to ten. Every time God says that for the sake of a few righteous people God will forgive the whole place.

The reason I say Abraham took an almost humanistic approach is it appears that Abraham, for some reason, did not want God to destroy those cities. I do not think Abraham was really concerned with the righteous getting caught in the crossfire, because I believe the above story suggests that Abraham did not really think anybody in the cities *was* righteous. Apparently there were less than ten, as the story ends with God raining fire and sulfur on both cities.

This story has led both Jewish and Christian scholars to argue that a few righteous people are the only reason existence continues. A Jewish legend refers to the Lamed Vav Tzaddikim—the Thirty-Six Righteous. According to the legend, every generation has thirty-six righteous people in it that stave off God's wrath, providing us with more time to appropriately respond to God's love. Christianity suggests something similar, inasmuch as God promises to not leave the world without a witness. That is, so Christian theology argues, if there were no witnesses to the Triune God then either the world would cease to exist or the lack of witnesses would simply prove that God does not exist. The suggestion is, therefore, that without the Dorothy Days, Oscar Romeros, and Sojourner Truths, space and time would end as there would be no one here reflecting either the promises or character of God.

I find such an account compelling. Is God's existence or, rather, the existence of creation, dependent on a few humans participating in the divine economy known as the Trinity? In the case of the former we must say no, because God does not need us to be God. God's existence is not contingent on our ongoing existence. In the case of the latter, however, I think we must say yes. If there were no witnesses to God, then the world would be lost, as we would no longer have the means to even know that we had been redeemed. Without the few embodying the way of Christ, how would we even know what Christ looks like? If there were no longer any saints, we would have to assume that the Holy Spirit, which Jesus said would be with us until the end of the age, had withdrawn itself from our presence.

I am not sure how convinced my students were of this theological account. Most of them like to presume that they are the righteous ones. Or they have been so flooded with Enlightenment individualism that they are offended by the very idea that someone like, for example, Daniel Berrigan may be the reason for their continued existence.

One of my students, however, felt that there could be a kernel of truth in this, but that I was wrong to extend it beyond certain geographical boundaries. That is, the student thought that we must stick to the notion that this only works for cities, not creation as a whole (though Sodom and Gomorrah is not the first time God destroyed a lot of people in a moment—the Flood, which, true enough, God promised never to impose again, was an act against all earth).

"Perhaps," I reluctantly concurred. "However, rather than focus on Las Vegas, let's think about the city of not just the United States but of an empire: Washington, D.C. In terms of corruption, pride, pomposity, greed, blood, murder, and idolatry, there is no city quite like this one. Now, why do you think this city continues to persist?"

One student simply said that he was an atheist and was therefore not obligated to go any further into my thought experiment. Another student, a young woman from the D.C. area, responded that within D.C., for all of its sinfulness (and what makes D.C. particularly viable is how it affects the rest of the world) happens to reside a handful of Christians who attempt to embody the oh-so-subversive Sermon on the Mount. She claimed that there were all sorts of radical people who constantly pray and protest against sin and corruption. Right in the capital of the American Empire, I was told, were all sorts of people wreaking holy havoc in the name of Christ.

Upon hearing this, and I had heard rumors of such holiness existing amid imperial chaos, I suggested that the only way to prove whether or not this account of the righteous preserving creation, or in this case, just a city, was true or not would require that all of these devout people relocate elsewhere (and, just to play it safe, not look back). My student immediately, and quite faithfully I think, protested, "But my parents live in D.C.!"

## Discussion Questions

Have you ever thought that, as a Christian, you may be slowing God's anger? Or kindling God's wrath?

Do you believe that God's patience can be extended due to the holiness of God's followers? Why or why not?

Who are those people you think have reflected the promises or character of God in such a way that this world has somehow benefited from their lives?

PART III

# Our Praise

## Introduction: Whose Liturgy? Which Holidays (Holy Days)?

**THE WORD** *holiday* is a combination of the two words *holy* and *day*. Holy means "to be set apart." Holiday, therefore, bears the connotations of a day set aside, or set apart, for religious purposes. The church has its own holy days/holidays that constitute its liturgical year, which include Advent, Christmas, Lent, and Easter (with a host of other holy days between).

These holy days (or holy seasons) serve to enact and reenact the story of Christianity so that its participants remember who they are in order to be who they are called to be. Holy days in the church are days set apart from other days to create a body of people set apart from the world. They are about the business of forming a certain kind of person: a disciple of Christ. The church is called to be holy, and that requires that the church be set apart from that which is not the church. The liturgical year, with its holy days, renders such holiness a possibility. Holy days are integral to the process of discipleship as the recognition of these days or seasons shape us to see the world in a way otherwise not possible.

The church, however, is not the only body politic that has its own liturgy. The nation-state also has a well-developed calendar predicated on creating a certain kind of person: a devout citizen. Many people in the United States celebrate a host of holy days that include Columbus Day, Memorial Day, Independence Day, Mother's Day, and Thanksgiving. These particular days were created to remind citizens of the United States who they are in order to be who the nation-state needs them to be. These days are set aside to form a kind of person not possible without these sacred days. The church and the state are about the same business: the creation of a particular kind of person for a specific kind of purpose.

Christians in the United States, in particular, have to contend with the conflation and merger of both the church's and the nation-state's holy days. This demands careful attention and begs many questions. What does it mean for Christians to celebrate Memorial Day or Thanksgiving? What does it "do" to us? How does it shape us in ways different from those who do not observe these holidays? Why do Christians, whose liturgy does not include Independence Day or Veterans Day, incorporate the state's holy days into church services? What does it mean for Christians to celebrate Christmas, Valentine's Day, and Easter in ways determined by the market that allow anyone of any or no faith commitment also to celebrate these holy days?

In this last section, I aim to problematize our participation in the state's liturgy in hopes of showing the difference between what makes one a Christian and what makes one, to speak crudely, an "American." The state enacts its own liturgy aimed at making us *its* disciples. The difficulty in our situation is that we have adopted many of the state's sacred rituals as our own and placed them in the center of our worship services. We have to examine how this shapes us so that we can better understand if it is Christianity narrating our understanding of the state, or if the state is narrating our understanding of Christianity.

The following chapters include conversations surrounding Memorial Day, Mother's Day, Christmas, Thanksgiving, and the observation of Martin Luther King Jr.'s birthday. I hope that by taking a closer look at these holidays we can gain a better sense of what it means to faithfully discern how they should form us.

Before discussing these holy days, it is important to begin this section with a prayer. It is appropriate to include prayer in our discussion of holidays because this exposes the confused testimony prevalent in our understanding of God. I fear that much of what passes for prayer belittles God—renders God trite. I, therefore, offer a prayer of lamentation spun satirically. The juxtaposition of the absurdity of our prayers with a call to enact justice is intentional. I only hope that you find it as offensive to read as I found it to write.

*Chapter Thirteen*

# A Simple Plea to the All-Powerful, All-Knowing and Entirely Beneficent God Who Really, Really Loves Sports (but not the Orioles or Some South Asians)

Dear God,

Could you please stop fixing sporting events? Seriously. Your unpredictability is killing me at the betting table. I can never figure out who you're helping. One moment you're hooking up a player with the Panthers and the next another player for the Cards. How am I supposed to figure out which one you love the most, or which one prayed the hardest that you would help them "guide" the ball to just the right place, if you keep flip-flopping? Could you be a little less fickle with your handouts?

You are, after all, immutable. That means you are unchanging. It says so right there in the Bible, Malachi 3:6: "For

I, the Lord, do not change." Yet when it comes to sports, I am far more consistent than you. I have been an Orioles fan since 1981. Other than that time where you clearly graced us in '83, do you know what misery I, along with other O's fans, have had to endure for decades? What do you have against Baltimore? It's no more pagan than any other city (though you do seem to be a little more generous to the Ravens—perhaps I should speak to the owner of the Orioles about requiring team prayer before each game?).

Anyway, do you think you could just pick a team and stay with them? No one likes a bandwagon fan. Actually, you're not just a fan, but you, if the winners of Super Bowls, World Cups, and World Series are to be believed, actually rig the games (and I thought the Patriot's coach was bad). I just thought I would ask. I assumed, since you are so concerned about touchdowns, homeruns, and last-second shots, you wouldn't mind.

Oh, another thing (sorry to be so needy): I know you are omnipotent, but it seems that you have been giving more attention to Sunday afternoon scores than to a few other things in the world. Granted, I know extremely affluent athletes who own multiple cars and houses are crucial to you, but do you think you could, oh, I don't know, do something about the ongoing genocide in Darfur? Tibet? Rwanda?

Perhaps you could send out a little help to ease the tensions between your followers in Israel and Palestine? There is also this AIDS epidemic occurring in Africa. Cancer is not good. Nor are SIDS, diabetes, blindness, paralysis, global warming, and the near-extinction of pandas, blue whales, monk seals, red wolves, or the mantled howler monkey (come on, those creatures are awesome).

Perhaps (I'm feeling a bit like Abraham here), perhaps you could tone down the number of tsunamis, earthquakes, and hurricanes you've been sending lately? While I'm asking, any chance you might convince your world leaders to stop making nuclear missiles? I know it's a longshot, but since all governments are ordained by you, I thought it wouldn't hurt to ask. Also, did you know that almost every four seconds someone dies of starvation? Of course you did. You're omniscient.

One last thing: Maybe you could look into why more than 2 billion people live on something like $2 a day. More than 500 million people in South Asia live (if you can call it that) on less than $1 a day. I mean, I hear all the time how you are obviously blessing the people in North America with a surplus of goods, so I know that means we're doing something right. I can't even count the number of "God Bless America" bumper stickers on the back of your average Lincoln, Lexus, or Mercedes. In a world where less than ten percent of the total population actually owns a car, many of us are so blessed as to be able to have numerous vehicles! How ungrateful are those that don't praise your name? But what did all those others do that was so bad to not garner your attention?

Don't get me wrong, I'm not questioning your justice; I'm sure their prayers for food and the basic necessities of life deserve to go unanswered. If I learned anything from the book of Job it is to tread quietly and not ask too many questions. But since you are overtly concerned with who wears Super Bowl rings, and Jesus did, after all, say that whatever we ask for you will provide . . . well . . . could you please make sure the Orioles get a better pitching staff next year? That would be my prayer: Just guide the ball straight and true into the catcher's mitt oh Lord. Straight and true.

Sincerely,
A distraught fan

## Discussion Questions

Many athletes point to the heavens when they do well as a form of gratitude—which could be a good thing. Yet, what is the point this satirical prayer is trying to make in light of these public acts of gratitude?

Can we really assume that God is concerned with sporting events when, literally, a billion people on this planet lack the basic necessities of life?

*Chapter Fourteen*

# I Don't want to be a Scrooge, but . . .

*And what about Ole Nick?*
*Turned out he was The Other Side.*
*Whenever the winter hits bottom*
*and the back-to-school buying levels off,*
*along comes Mammon with that Red-Nosed Reindeer*
*and retail sales go up thirty points.*
—Henderson Nylrod (John Howard Yoder)

*The history of Christianization is to be welcomed as a success story. Better a superficial Christianity than none at all. Better a government saying "in God we trust" and not meaning it than not even saying it. Better replace the sun god by the Son of God than the sun worship go on undiluted.*
—John Howard Yoder

**LEST THE SARCASM BE LOST ON US**, the above quotes, both by Mennonite theologian John Howard Yoder, are intended to be quite caustic. He is, sardonically, suggesting that it is all too easy to replace Christian discipleship with the inevitable compromise that comes from Christians wanting to have their Jesus and their wealth/health/power, too. This is surely evident in Christianity's co-opting of Christmas with a free market mentality. Yet perhaps it goes beyond such an adulteration of this holy day. What if it is the case that Christmas is itself something of a co-opting of secularism?

Each year it is customary to hear Christians lament the demise of the "true meaning" of Christmas. Many in the church complain about the unbridled materialism displayed during the holiday season and that this has taken Christ out of Christmas. While it may be true that the celebration of Jesus' birth has become synonymous with consumerism, avarice, and gluttony, the real problem, nevertheless, remains hidden. It is not that Christ is no longer in Christmas; rather, perhaps Christ never *was* in Christmas.

To say Christ never was in Christmas is not a particularly eccentric claim. No complicated exegetical moves are needed to reinforce such a statement. The celebration of the birth of Jesus simply has no foundation in Scripture or the early church tradition. Beyond this, the very idea of Christmas—especially as it now occurs in our culture—would have been simply unthinkable in the first three centuries of Christianity. Christmas was not celebrated until the middle of the fourth century and was originally titled the Feast of the Nativity. Most historians argue that it originated as a substitute for pagan celebrations of the winter solstice. Not knowing the precise date of Jesus' birth, the Roman Catholic Church opted for December 25 as the day for the Feast of the Nativity in order, perhaps, to lend Christian meaning to already existent pagan rituals. Rather than honor the sun god, the church introduced festivities to commemorate the birth of the Son of God.

This, in and of itself, may not have been a terribly bad idea. It should be considered a good thing when those under God's providence decide to no longer honor pagan rituals. However, does the attempt to replace pagan rituals with Christian rituals only legitimize the rituals in the first place? Isn't this just the acceptance of paganism under a delicate coating of Christian terminology? December 25 may now be a day commemorating Jesus' birth (as opposed to the sun god), but how does such a re-narration not run the risk of being defined by the antecedent practice?

This seems to be a tricky area for some Christians—especially Anabaptists. Maybe for some Protestants and Catholics it is permissible to accept this holiday as a replacement for pagan rituals. Yet would such a thing be possible if Christianity had not been the state religion? If our basic approach to Christianity is non-Constantinian, then shouldn't we question not just how the holiday is celebrated but the holiday itself? Celebrating the birth of Christ is one thing (and one thing that must be done in awareness of the thousands of babies, the "Holy innocents," slaughtered because of it), yet how do we, as Anabaptists, participate in this "holiday," given the kind of socio-political formation that made it possible?

The larger problem, therefore, seems to be the implementation of this holy day in the life of the polis. To render the birth of Jesus an event that becomes a part of the life of all society—regardless of faith content—turns Christianity into a civil religion. How is it consistent to reject the Constantinian compromise in matters related to church membership, war, the state—yet completely ignore how it constructed and manipulated feast days? After all of these years, Christmas still exists to serve the government. For those of us who now reside in a liberal capitalist state, Christianity is used as a pawn to bolster its economy. Public schools are closed and malls keep longer hours—all in an effort to profit on the birth of the world's savior.

For the descendents of the Radical Reformation, a legitimate defense of the celebration of Christmas is in order. By this I do not simply mean the justification for such a practice; rather, what is essential is the realization that, as we wish to elevate primitive Christianity as the paradigmatic form over and above Christianity after Constantine, Christmas, as it has come to us, may be a bad idea. To critique how Christmas is celebrated, as mentioned earlier, is neither a new thing nor a very difficult thing to do. To ask *why* Christmas is celebrated may be a more daunting and, understandably so, unpopular task. Whether or not Christmas is the product of the early medieval church's struggle to Christianize the Roman Empire is an argument open to debate. Unfortunately, such a debate is a much-neglected one.

If anything is to be celebrated, it is the incarnation—for this is what the birth of Jesus represents. John Howard Yoder writes: "Not the innocence of the infant but the obedience of the Man, Jesus, saves us."[24] Of course, the incarnation is an ongoing event, one that leads Jesus—along with his followers—to a cross. That it leads us, instead, to department stores should raise a few eyebrows. That it has so successfully formed us into shoppers only tells the tale that the state, alongside the ever-expanding market, has been far more formative than Scripture.

Originally published as "Why Christmas?" *The Mennonite* 6.24, December 13, 2003, pp. 12-13.

## Discussion Questions:

York suggests that the annual cries of "putting Christ back into Christmas" are fallacious because, historically (at least for the first 300 years of Christianity) there was no celebration of the birth of Christ. Indeed, the creation of Christmas, as a substitute for a pagan holiday, was a way of forcing citizens of the empire to come to mass. Yet now it is a part of our liturgical year as well as a civil holiday. How do we maintain this recognition of Christ's birth in a way that does justice to the story of Christianity in light of its origin?

How does the celebration of Christmas in North America reflect a co-opting of church and state? Is this a good or a bad thing? Why?

How can Christians reclaim Christmas as a significant part of their liturgical year that shows the world the incarnation? That is, what practices must we engage that reveal to the world God in Jesus?

What does shopping, and the economy it serves, have to do with the birth of the Jewish messiah?

*Chapter Fifteen*

# Turkey, Genocide, and the Eucharist: An Argument for Fasting on Thanksgiving

*Considering that virtually none of the standard fare surrounding Thanksgiving contains an ounce of authenticity, historical accuracy, or cross-cultural perception, why is it so apparently ingrained? Is it necessary to the American psyche to perpetually exploit and debase its victims to justify its history?*
—Michael Dorris

**OF ALL THE HOLIDAYS** that both the United States and the church celebrate, perhaps none is quite so mired in confusion as Thanksgiving. Our history books paint us pictures of pilgrims and "Indians" (this is, still, not India) surrounding a large picnic table sharing the goods that both brought to the meal. Of course, most of us are by now aware of the fictitious nature of many myths of Thanksgiving. One of the most self-serving myths suggests that the English and Natives were great friends. It was only a mere generation after the so-called first Thanksgiving of 1621 that the vast majority of Natives in the New England area had either fled to Canada, been sold into slavery, or massacred by the English.

To even refer to this autumn meal as the first Thanksgiving is anachronistic. The history of Thanksgiving is quite muddled and only becomes solidified as a national holy day centuries after 1621. First President George Washington proclaimed a Thanksgiving in December 1777 to pay homage to their victory over the British at Saratoga. President John Adams declared Thanksgiving in 1798 and 1799, while Thomas Jefferson spent his tenure as president without declaring a day set aside for giving thanks. President James Madison not only set apart a day for thanksgiving at the close of the War of 1812 but declared the holiday twice in the year 1815. These days of commemoration had nothing to do with "Indians and Pilgrims," nor were they even celebrated in November. Thanksgiving does not become a fixed national holiday to be annually celebrated in November until President Abraham Lincoln established it in 1863. Even then, it underwent another shift when President Franklin Roosevelt, in 1939, moved Thanksgiving up a week to bolster a depressed economy.[25]

This brief venture into the history of Thanksgiving is not, however, the aim of this chapter. What I am more concerned about is what it is Christians celebrate when we recognize Thanksgiving as a holy day. Though it has become, harmless enough, a time set aside for families to get together to eat a lot of food, watch a lot of football and give a lot of thanks, we must ask the question, What is it that Christians are being grateful for?

Before the European invasion of the Americas, conservative estimates suggest that there were 30 to 50 million Native Americans occupying what is now known as the United States (some estimates go beyond 100 million). There are now only 2 million or so Natives in the United States. Where did they go? As the comedian Chris Rock so eloquently put it on one of his comedy tours: "Everybody wants to save the trees. The trees? I see trees everywhere! When's the last time you saw two Indians?" It would be funny if it were not so true.

There are several reasons for the almost complete annihilation of the various tribes of Native Americans. The most brutal include the conquering of Natives through violence, starvation, and plagues—all introduced by Europeans. King James praised God for sending the plagues amongst the savages, and what God failed to do the U.S. Calvary completed by introducing smallpox to Natives and relegating the remaning ones to reservations incapable of nurturing life.[26] Few have suffered more at the hands of the "white man" (and woman) than Native Americans, yet each year we celebrate Thanksgiving as if God blessed us for coming over and introducing so much misery and oppression to its native peoples.

When the Wampanoags were asked by the Massachusetts Department of Commerce in 1970 to select a speaker to mark 350 years since the pilgrims landed, they chose the late Frank James. Though his name was anglicized, he forever remained a Native American (he was known as Wampsutta by his own people). Due to concerns of the white people in charge of the ceremony, James was asked to present a copy of his speech before he was allowed to read it. What follows below is a partial glimpse:

> It is with mixed emotion that I stand here to share my thoughts. . . . It is with a heavy heart that I look back upon what happened to my people. Even before the Pilgrims landed it was common practice for explorers to capture Indians, take them to Europe and sell them as slaves for 220 shillings apiece. The Pilgrims had hardly explored the shores of Cape Cod for four days before they had robbed the graves of my ancestors and stolen their corn and beans. . . . Massasoit, the great Sachem of the Wampanoag, knew these facts, yet he and his people welcomed and befriended the settlers of the Plymouth Plantation. . . . This action by Massasoit was perhaps our biggest mistake. We, the Wampanoag, welcomed you, the white man, with open arms, little knowing that it was the beginning of the end; that before 50 years were to pass, the Wampanoag would no

> longer be a free people. What happened in those short 50 years? What has happened in the last 300 years? History gives us facts and there were atrocities; there were broken promises—and most of these centered around land ownership. . . . We forfeited our country. Our lands have fallen into the hands of the aggressor. We have allowed the white man to keep us on our knees. What has happened cannot be changed, but today we must work toward a more humane America, a more Indian America were people and nature once again are important.[27]

Though there was nothing in his speech that was false, he was not allowed to present it. Truth was not a welcomed component of the white people's celebration of the European invasion. What they would remember would be what they wanted to remember—even if it was nothing but lies.

Even when it does not benefit us, perhaps *especially* when it does not benefit us, Christians are to be truth-tellers. Our settlement in this country was only possible due to the enslavement and massacring of its natives. We all have blood on our hands. This does not mean that we are to live lives of perpetual guilt because of our heritage, but it does require that we live lives that enact justice, that attempt to find solidarity toward those we have for so long wronged. I admit, I am not entirely sure what such justice would look like. I imagine we would need to leave that up to Native Americans.

What I do know, or at least think I know, is that our celebration of Thanksgiving Day must take a different shape. Christians only have one true thanksgiving celebration and that is the Eucharist. The Eucharist means thanksgiving, and it is in our feeding on the broken body of Jesus that should enable us to better understand those bodies that were broken in order for us to be where we are today. This is not to equate the sacrifice of Jesus with the sacrifice of natives; rather, because we feed on a broken savior, we have the resources to better name those who have been, likewise, broken.

I think that the most interesting, the most counter-cultural, the most subversive thing a Christian could do on Thanksgiving would be to fast. After fasting as a means of protesting the lies that have become a part of the mythos of the birth of this nation, we could cap the day off by celebrating the Eucharist. Perhaps then we might find a way to truthfully move forward in regards to our past with our native brothers and sisters.

Originally published in *Christian Ethics Today*, issue 80, vol. 17, no. 4, Fall 2010, pp. 9-10.

## Discussion Questions

Is it a problem that Christians in North America celebrate Thanksgiving? What are reasons for celebrating it? Against? Why does York imagine fasting to be an appropriate response to the United State's celebration of Thanksgiving?

How does the Lord's Supper demand that we be truth-tellers? How does our participation in the ultimate act of thanksgiving, the flesh and blood of Jesus, require that we think about the ongoing mistreatment of Native Americans?

President Abraham Lincoln used language in the Bible when in 1863 he established Thanksgiving as a holiday. Lincoln was very frank about the country's sin. He called on the American people to set apart a day of Thanksgiving and praise "to our beneficent Father who dwelleth in the Heavens." He also recommended "penitence for our national perverseness and disobedience, commend to His tender care all those who have become widows, orphans, mourners, or sufferers in the lamentable civil strife. . . . "[28] What might have been the motivation behind the president's comments? How might this make Thanksgiving a different holiday than once perceived? Does this statement begin to help "tell the truth" about Thanksgiving?

*Chapter Sixteen*

# DETHRONING A KING

*A dangerous Negro, now a national hero. How shall we work with that?*

—Vincent Harding

**IN A BRIEF ESSAY** entitled *Martin Luther King Jr.: Dangerous Prophet*, Vincent Harding, a colleague of King, reminds his readers that as easy as it is to forget that Jesus was an executed criminal who undermined the very politics that makes this fallen world turn, so too is it both easy and tempting to twist King into our own image of one who is no longer a prophet—but an idol that serves rather than questions our interests.[29]

In 1963, Martin Luther King Jr. was called the most dangerous Negro in the United States because he posed a threat to the very precious ideals that, unfortunately, continue to underwrite our socio-economic and political culture. This same man is now revered as a national saint. The question that must be asked is this: Did we undergo the changes that King demanded—an alternative economy, the practice of nonviolence, and the ceasing of imperialism? Or has his message somehow changed since his death so that it can accommodate that which he gave his life to in protest?

For instance, how is it possible for a man who once preached against the evils of capitalism to be awarded heroic status in a capitalist culture? How is it possible that a person who decried the wickedness that is war is remembered as a patriotic saint in the world's strongest warring machine? How is it that a Christian pastor, who so intuitively understood how racism, classism, and militarism go hand-in-hand, is remembered as an icon in a culture perpetually divided by these oppressive horrors?

Finally, how is it possible that organizations such as General Motors, Tommy Hilfiger, Exxon, Coca-Cola, Disney, Wal-Mart, and McDonalds, top purveyors of Western imperialism, were major benefactors for a $100-plus million memorial in his name? This is, ironically, a memorial that will be placed in a city known throughout the world as having a serious homeless problem. Would King not be appalled by the very idea of spending so much money on a monument *in his name* in D.C., while countless people in that same city go to bed cold and hungry? Is this memorial actually talking about the same Martin Luther King Jr. who argued that the United States, if it is to achieve equality, requires a completely restructured economy (in his words, a "modified socialism")? Will this memorial serve to remind us of who King is, or, in its very use of such vast economic resources, will its very existence actually make it easier to forget who he really was?

Apparently the King so often touted today is not the same man as the King of 1963. For the King who was hated and eventually assassinated for his dangerous and subversive ideals (that is, standing with the oppressed), has now become a part of the very machine he protested. In a sense, it is pure brilliance on the part of the empire. The best way to deal with a dangerous radical like King is to domesticate him. Claim him. Say you love him. Give him a national "holy" day, and in so doing stand free from any claims he might have upon us.

Then he will no longer stand above the American people holding us accountable for jingoist practices. He will no longer stand apart demanding that we restructure our society so that there need not be any poor among us. Rather, we have become exactly that which he was attempting to avoid: richer yet poorer, except that now we justify this in his name.

King had no interest in liberating minorities so that they could simply participate in the evils that white people had perfected; instead, he wanted to overturn the entire edifice so that all people could practice justice, charity, and love toward one another.

But now, warring presidents gleefully quote him, "supporters" cash in on his name, and the largest capitalist corporations on the planet support the building of a monument that, it seems, only the wealthy could truly enjoy. For what will starving poor persons think about as they peer at the expensive image of Martin Luther King Jr.? I imagine they will think that the "King" is dead.

This was originally published in *Christian Ethics Today*, Vol. 14, No. 1, 2008, pp. 18-19.

## Discussion Questions

What do you think of the ironies presented in this chapter? Name them, and then ask yourself this question: What makes the recognition of King's life so problematic for those who *truly* want to honor him?

Do you think that King has been domesticated? How so, and for what purpose? How can we reclaim him?

What should an appropriate remembrance of King look like in our churches? How would that look different from the way the nation-state remembers him?

*Chapter Seventeen*

# Who Mourns the Gods? Part 2: A Memorial Day Reflection

**IN THE FIRST PART** of this two-part set of essays, I attempted to draw connections between the reasons for *disbelief* in the divinity of Apollo with many of our reasons for *belief* in the god of North American Christianity. That is, was Apollo rejected because he asked too much by desiring that we worship him? Granted, it is of utmost importance for Christians to reject false gods, yet that is precisely what was at stake when I compared the Enterprise's rejection of Apollo with our predominant culture's acceptance of Jesus. My fear in the prior essay was that the very reasons for *not* considering Apollo worthy of worship are the very reasons why we *do* think Jesus is worthy of worship. Apollo demanded subservience, obedience, fidelity, and ownership of our bodies. Jesus wants nothing less.

But how do we discern between false gods and the God above all other gods? In this time of honoring the sacrifices made by those who serve both "God and Country," it is important to be able to answer the above question well. Perhaps an example of a few other Greek gods and their connection to the god of "God and Country" will help.

As I watched the Star Trek episode, I was intrigued by the possibility of a return to the pagan gods. This is not completely unheard of, as there are a number of Greek and Roman cults still dedicated to Zeus and other gods of antiquity. I do not, however, imagine that a widespread return of Zeus, Athena, and Hermes is going to take place. Nor would I desire such an event. The problem with the Greek gods is that they were too much like us. They were capricious, fickle, violent, vindictive, and not trustworthy. They needed to go.

However, what if they were to make a return in the form of a different god? Would we notice? I am not speaking literally of course; consider this a poetic or metaphorical exercise. Take, for example, the Greco-Roman god Dionysus. Dionysus, also known as Bacchus, was the god of wine who inspired ecstatic celebrations through the partaking of fermented grapes. This was understood as a form of liberation. Under the influence of wine, one was freed from both one's own self and cultural taboos designed to restrict behavior some argued was simply natural for humans. Inhibitions were lost, and one could descend, or, rather, for the follower of Dionysus, *ascend* into a state of madness—at least in terms of ordinary behavior.

We know that Jesus' first miracle was the turning of water into wine. We also know that wine is a prevalent drink in both the Old and the New Testament, a gift from God. The writer of Ecclesiastes tells us to drink our wine with a merry heart (9:7), and that we shall plant vineyards and drink wine as an act of celebration from our exilic existence (Amos 9:14). Yet we also know that, for the disciple of Jesus, the kind of madness that follows intoxication is not liberatory or to be celebrated; rather, it is condemned as behavior not exemplary of holiness (Rom. 13:13, 1 Cor. 6:10, 1 Peter 4:3-4).

The question that Christians who enjoy the taste of wine must ask is, Do we find freedom in ecstasy of alcohol or in the path of Jesus? The latter does not rule out drinking alcohol, but it does rule out the destruction of the temple that is the body (this being the case, our unbridled consumption of food can be more problematic than wine). Therefore, one can gain a sense to whom we belong based on, to use this comparison, how we respond to the question of wine drinking. Which deity do we worship: Dionysus or Jesus?

Though such a comparison requires a bit of creative liberty, I am convinced such an example works because Christians engage in those activities imagined to radiate the character of God. That is, if you find yourself giving aid to the poor, it is because you think that God is one who cares for the poor. If you are a Christian who refuses to help the poor, it is because you assume that such help doesn't indicate who God is and so isn't necessary.

I think such an exercise can work in a variety of situations. For instance, which "god" do we worship based on our response to our nation's enemies (and by nation I am referring to the nation-state, not the church). When Christians submit their bodies, as in the military, to learn how to wound, kill, assassinate and, if need be, completely destroy their enemies, they do so because they imagine that God not only endorses such behavior but would do so as well—even in the form of Jesus. Hence the importance of the question: What would Jesus do? A Christian serving in the military has already answered this question by imagining that Jesus would pick up guns, grenades, or knives in order to resist, beat into submission, and eliminate enemies. Christian soldiers *must* think this about Jesus, otherwise they would not, nor could not, serve in the military. If Jesus would not shoot, maim, or kill his enemy, then the Christian, as one who follows and imitates Jesus, cannot engage in this behavior either.

This is quite the conundrum for Christians because many of us are convinced that we not only have a stake in the survival, by any means necessary, of this and other nation-states, but that the God of Jesus favors and privileges in particular the United States. What once was reserved for Jews and Christians now belongs to the citizens of the United States: We imagine such citizenship makes us the new chosen people. Such a theological heresy, as espoused by politicians, written on our money, and recited in the pledge of allegiance, makes it difficult to discern any problem with the systematic training to kill enemies. The practices of the military are in no way antithetical to that of Christ; indeed, Christ, apparently, rules by military force. If only those select Jews who refused Christ in the first century had understood what we figured out—Jesus really is a mighty King David who rules by the sword!

Such thinking is commonplace among Christians in North America despite the fact that the prophets foretell the coming of one who will put an end to war (Isa. 2:4, Micah 4:3). Somehow such thinking looks past Jesus' (and Paul's) own comments as to how differently his followers will treat enemies:

> "But I tell you who hear me: Love your enemies, do good to those who hate you, bless those who curse you, pray for those who mistreat you." (Luke 6:27-28)
>
> "You have heard it that it was said, 'An eye for an eye and a tooth for a tooth.' But I say to you, Do not resist an evildoer. But if anyone strikes you on the right cheek, turn the other also. . . . You have heard that it was said, 'You shall love your neighbor and hate your enemy.' But I say to you, Love your enemies and pray for those who persecute you, so that you may be children of your Father in heaven." (Matt. 5:38-39, 43-45a)
>
> Bless those who persecute you; bless and do not curse. (Rom. 12:14)
>
> We work hard with our own hands. When we are cursed, we bless; when we are persecuted, we endure it. (1 Cor. 4:12)
>
> Do not repay anyone evil for evil. Be careful to do what is right in the eyes of everybody. If it is possible, as far as it depends on you, live at peace with everyone. Do not take revenge, my friends, but leave room for God's wrath, for it is written: "It is mine to avenge; I will repay," says the Lord. On the contrary: "If your enemy is hungry, feed him; if he is thirsty, give him something to drink. In doing this, you will heap burning coals on his head." Do not be overcome by evil, but overcome evil with good. (Rom. 12:17-21)

> Do not repay evil with evil or insult with insult, but with blessing, because to this you were called so that you may inherit a blessing. (1 Pet. 3:9)
>
> "Blessed are the peacemakers, for they will be called children of God." (Matt. 5:9)
>
> Then Jesus said to him, "Put your sword back into its place; for all who take the sword shall perish by the sword." (Matt. 26:52)

Regardless of what hermeneutical tactic one uses to interpret Scripture, one thing is clear: Christians are called to embody an ethic different from others in relating to enemies. Indeed, the very heart of what makes Christianity so unusual, so odd, perhaps so subversive, is its understanding of its enemies. Jesus has given us a new way to deal with our foes: to forgive them.

Yet this is not how the larger world views the situation. Enemies must be named and dealt with accordingly. For some, this includes the torture of waterboarding while for others it necessitates the terror of hanging nuclear missiles over the heads of other countries. Whatever war is, and it is many things, those soldiers who valiantly and sacrificially risk their lives for others only do so by their ability and willingness to slay whoever is in their way. Given that Jesus died for his enemies, was killed by them, and demanded that his followers pick up their cross and do likewise, my worry is that those who imagine a Jesus willing to bless their rifles and bayonets see him as having more in common with the Greek god Ares than Jesus of Nazareth. Ares was the god of war and bloodlust (the Romans referred to him as the god Mars). He engaged in war after war and was involved in one bloody conflict after another—all, of course, justified by his own logic.

Those who engaged in war during the reign of Ares looked to him for help. They looked to him (along with his more strategically minded half-sister Athena) for blessings on their noble crusades. There was never a shortage of justifiable causes for engaging in war, and Ares' name was often on the lips of those plunging their swords into other bodies or dying at the hands of another. Their sacrifice well may have been noble, and for that, along with soldiers of all stripes, we may honor their heroism.

Yet Christians are not called to be heroes. We are not the Clint Eastwoods, Rambos, and Achilles' of the world. We are called out to be those who would offer an alternative to never-ending incessant warring that the generals and politicos declare are our lot in life.Though there may always be warring in this world, just like adultery and theft, we are not called to participate. We know that there are no acts of redemptive violence or sacrifice because Christ's resurrection trumps the need for us to continue killing to preserve ourselves or third-party innocents.

When I think about the question of who mourns the gods, especially on this liturgical holy day that belongs to the nation-state, my thoughts go not to Apollo but to Ares. Why, in such a thoroughly Christian culture as ours does Jesus, the *Prince of Peace*, look so much like Ares, the *god of war*? Why do Christians confuse the two? And why do Christians continue to celebrate those willing to kill when Micah is very clear that we are to beat our swords into plowshares; and Jesus, very matter of factly I might add, states that those who live by the sword shall die by the sword? Why is Memorial Day, that day when the spoils of war are glorified, celebrated in our churches? These are the kinds of questions we must ask if we are to be truthful about which god is being worshipped in our churches. I'd guess the ultimate question is not whether Ares has returned; rather, the question is, Did Ares ever leave?

## Discussion Questions

This chapter ends with a series of questions to be addressed. Is it correct to suggest that our interpretation of God has more in line with Ares than Jesus? Why or why not?

See Micah 3:10-4:8. Many times this text is read during the Lord's Supper. Why would this scripture be so important to read around the table of our Lord? What does this passage have to say about the celebration of a secular nation's fallen heroes?

Think about why Memorial Day is celebrated in some of our churches. Then try to address the significance of this holy day in light of the radical approach to our enemies Jesus commands us to take. What does it mean to either celebrate Memorial Day or refuse to recognize it?

Compare a Memorial Day celebration with a typical Sunday that celebrates the life, death, and resurrection of Jesus. What are the key differences?

What does the death and resurrection of Jesus mean in relation to the notion of redemptive acts of violence? That is, the "heroes'" of this culture are celebrated for participating in acts of violence that allow us to maintain a certain kind of life. Should we be rethinking any way of life preserved through the willingness of our young to kill and be killed?

*Chapter Eighteen*

# Mother Mary

**IN HIS BOOK** *A Community of Character*, Stanley Hauerwas argues that the first enemy of the family is the church.[30] Hauerwas' provocative claim stems from both Scripture and his reading of Plato, who argued that the first enemy of the state was the family. In terms of the latter, Plato understood that biological ties could threaten the good of the republic if a citizen's loyalty was first to the family and then second to the *polis* (the Greek city-state). Any citizen willing to love family more than state was a threat to the social harmony of the state. A good citizen must be capable of making sacrifices, and sometimes those sacrifices demand that we love the state more than the family.

Plato's understanding of the overarching importance of the state is difficult for many of us to hear. The family is all but deified in our present culture. Many churches present themselves as "family friendly" to tell potential members that what is really important is family. Yet a quick perusal of Jesus' sayings on family makes it difficult to reconcile our glorification of the biological family:

> "Whoever comes to me and does not hate father and mother, wife and children, brothers and sisters, yes, and even life itself, cannot be my disciple." (Luke 14:26)

> "And everyone who has left houses or brothers or sisters or father or mother or wife or children or fields, for my name's sake, will receive a hundredfold, and will inherit eternal life." (Matt. 19:29)
>
> "Do not think that I have come to bring peace on the earth; I have not come to bring peace, but a sword. For I have come to set a man against his father, and a daughter against her mother, and a daughter-in-law against her mother-in-law; and one's foes will be the members of one's own household. Whoever loves father or mother more than me is not worthy of me; and whoever loves son or daughter more than me is not worthy of me." (Matt. 10:34-37)
>
> Then his mother and his brothers came; and standing outside, they sent to him and called him. A crowd was sitting around him; and they said to him "Your mother and brothers and sisters are outside asking for you." And he replied, "Who are my mother and my brothers?" And looking about on those who were sitting around him Jesus said, "Look! Here are my mother and my brothers. Whoever does the will of God is my brother and sister and mother." (Mark 3:31-35)

These are not exactly ringing endorsements of our culture's fetish with family values. Many are tempted to look at these passages and suggest that what Jesus is really saying is that we have to get our priorities right. But this is not what Jesus is saying (otherwise he would have said it). Jesus is not talking about our priorities, but, as Hauerwas argues, this is about living in a new age where "everything has been returned to its original purpose."[31] Rather than attempt to domesticate Jesus' comments on the family to fit our preconceptions of what a family is, we should attempt to understand them eschatologically. That is, how do we interpret Jesus' comments on family in light of our living in a new age?

One thing we can say is that the family is certainly good—but it is not the highest good. The chief end of all flesh is the worship of the triune God. This end relativizes all other commitments—whether to the market, the state, or the family. Even the atheist Bertrand Russell pointed out that Christianity, at best, has a rather ambivalent attitude toward the family: "'Who so loveth father or mother more than me is not worthy of me,' we read in the Gospels, and this means, in effect, that a man should do what he thinks right, even if his parents think it wrong—the view to which an ancient Roman . . . would not subscribe."[32]

Though Russell incorrectly sees this as the catalyst for the development of the individual conscience, what Russell does understand is that early Christians had a loyalty that went beyond the biological family: the church. This was, of course, detrimental to the family as well as the state because it was assumed that a strong state begins with a strong family. The early Christians were viewed as subversive for a number of reasons, one of which was their ability to forsake their mothers and fathers, their brothers and sisters, even sometimes their children, for the sake of discipleship. It is not that they did not love their families; rather, they had a different conception of the family. It was a conception that went beyond the parameters of biology and bloodlines and was determined by baptism. Baptism inaugurated a new family. This new and eschatological family might *include* the biological family but would not be *defined* by it. "Who are my mother and brothers?" Jesus asks. "Only those who do the will of God."

Somewhere along the line, the church in North America thought it a good idea to honor mothers with their own holy day. Though Mother's Day has an interesting and long history throughout the world, this recent development now occupies a day set aside in the liturgical calendars of most churches. Many churches underwrite this celebration with a reference to the command to honor thy mother (as well as Father's Day with honor thy father). I think the honoring of our mothers *should* be considered an important facet of our ecclesial life. I only hope we can come to a more faithful understanding of who our mothers really are so that we can treat this day consistent with the politics of the baptized family.

One way to do this is to remember and claim as our mother the mother of Jesus, Mary. We honor Mary, the *theotokos* (the God-bearer), not because she was the biological mother of Jesus but because she was obedient to God. Therefore, just like any baptized woman in church history, Mary really *is* our mother. If Mother's Day is to have a place in our churches, let it not be a mawkish glorification of biology but the celebration of the fact that a Christian has many mothers—as well as fathers, sons and daughters, brothers and sisters. Let it be a day that reminds us of our eschatological family in the past, the present, and the future.

## Discussion Questions

York claims that Mary, the mother of Jesus, is also the mother of all of us. Yet this motherhood is extended to all baptized women. How does this make sense?

How do biological families differ from baptismal families? Think about the passages of Scripture mentioned in the text and then ask, Which family (biological or baptismal) takes precedence?

Based on this article, what is a potential problem with "family friendly" churches?

Should the church cease celebrating Mother's (and Father's) Day? How would you justify keeping this practice? How would such a celebration need to change to reflect the radical nature of our baptisms?

# EPILOGUE OR EULOGY?

**I HAVE ALWAYS WANTED** Soren Kierkegaard, that wonderfully distraught (only because he cared so much) Danish Christian, to write an afterword for one of my books. It is probably never going to happen, as he died in 1855. Therefore I have decided to take some liberties with his namesake as well as his work. Since an afterword written by the "Great Dane" is impossible, I have written an epilogue that reveals how important his work is for those of us living in a devoutly Christian—yet also post-Christian—nation. I offer this epilogue not to provide one more criticism of Christianity in America but to challenge my readers (and more importantly myself) to think through what it means to long for any Christian nation other than the Christian nation that is the church.

Kierkegaard understood well the danger of everything becoming Christian. He worried that inasmuch as everything becomes Christian, Christianity ceases to exist. This is not to say that he was not concerned with evangelism or spreading the gospel; rather, he understood too well how difficult it really is to deny one's self and take up a cross. I do not want to say that he was pessimistic about human nature; he just did not share our culture's unbridled optimism about human progress.

It was on this very point, the conflation of human

progress with the cross of Christ, that he thought was a turning away from truth. Jesus was a dirty, ragged, homeless person with no place to rest his head, and yet he now looks so handsome, so well-dressed, so pristine, so healthy as he rules our affluent churches. It is with what I hope, therefore, would be Kierkegaard's kind posthumous permission that I offer you my version of his *A eulogy upon the human race or a proof that the New Testament is no longer truth.*[33]

## The Fate of Christendom (with apologies to Soren K.)

In the New Testament, Jesus the Christ, the one who, it is said, has redeemed all of creation, represents the situation in this manner: "For the gate is narrow and the road is hard that leads to life, and there are few who find it" (Matt. 7:14).

Ah, but on the contrary, Oh Lord. To speak only of the United States, you should know that we are all Christians. Do you not see that the way is as broad as it can possibly be? It must be, for it is the way that most of us walk. Why, you cannot even be an elected official unless you swear an oath on the Bible. We are all going, en masse, through the widest gate ever created. It is the gate of Christianity, and we all march along, spreading our gospel to the east, to make sure that the gate grows even wider (if, of course, all would but become like us).

Therefore, Oh Lord, your words are no longer truth.

All praise and glory belongs to the human race! Unfortunately, Oh Lord, the One who many have proclaimed as the savior of the world, you entertained a far too lowly notion of the human race. You failed to see the sublime heights by which we can attain if we but only pursue perfection in the most steady fashion. Progress is inevitable. *We* have progressed.

To that degree, Oh Lord, what you said in the New Testament is no longer truth. The way, our way, is the broadest, the gate is the widest, and all of us are Christians. According to some theologians, even those who are not Christian are, as long as they act like us, "anonymously" Christian. As a matter of fact, I dare to venture that our Jewish, Buddhist, and even atheist brothers and sisters that dwell among us are to a certain degree Christian—at least to the degree that we are all Christians, and in that degree are your words no longer truth. But Christian we all are.

Such an epiphany is surely dazzling. Think of the long way we have come. I grow almost dizzy at the thought of it. Oh Lord, the savior of the world, the redeemer of all creation, did you not inquire as to whether or not, upon your return, you would find faith on earth? (Luke 18:8). You surely had no idea, did you? How your expectations have been surpassed! How enthralling it must be to know that the human race would render your words false! Oh Lord, you must be proud to know that humanity has lived beyond your expectations. We forgive you for thinking so little of us. It is understandable; after all, we did so long ago put you to death. But now, you live freely among us. Evidence is all around. You are alive, and there are, at any given moment, more than one billion of us to prove it. We are living evidence as to how far we have come in the past 2000 years. Your words may no longer be truth, but isn't the world better for it?

# Notes

1. Cf. Sam Harris' *The End of Faith: Religion, Terror, and The Future of Reason* (New York: W. W. Norton & Co., 2005) as well as his *Letter to a Christian Nation* (New York: Vintage Books, 2008); Richard Dawkins' *The God Delusion* (Boston: Houghton Mifflin Company, 2006); and Christopher Hitchens' *God Is Not Great: How Religion Poisons Everything* (New York: Hachette Book Group, 2007).

2. Tertullian, *The Flesh of Christ* in *Ante-Nicene Fathers*, ed. Alexander Roberts and James Donaldson (1885; repr. Peabody: Hendrickson Publishers, 1999), 3:525.

3. Parthenogenesis does occur in various plants and species in the animal kingdom. Some species of insects, bees, and sharks are capable of parthenogenesis as well as Komodo Dragons and the whipped-tail lizard. Given that humans are not capable of this act makes the case of Mary miraculous. This, of course, renders it a moment within history that goes beyond what we currently know about nature.

4. John Milbank, *Theology and Social Theory: Beyond Secular Reason* (Oxford: Blackwell Publishers, 1999), 381.

5. Thomas of Celano, *Saint Francis of Assisi* (Chicago: Franciscan Herald Press, 1988), 273.

6. Ibid., 273-274.

7. Christopher Hitchens, *God Is Not Great*, 34.

8. Though he only refers to Francis on two occasions in this book, he has more openly ridiculed him, and the church that honors him, in televised interviews.

9. For a more detailed account of Clarence Jordan and the political witness of his life see my *Living on Hope While Living in Babylon: The Christian Anarchists of the Twentieth Century* (Eugene: Wipf & Stock, 2009). This article stems from my work in that book.

10. Ed. Jim Wallis and Joyce Hollyday, *Cloud of Witnesses* (Maryknoll: Orbis Books, 2006), 60.

11. This is recounted in James McClendon's *Biography as Theology: How Life's Stories Can Remake Theology* (Philadelphia: Trinity Press, 1990), 91.

12. Clarence Jordan, *The Cotton Patch Version of Paul's Epistles* (New York: Association Press, 1968), 99. Jordan's cotton patch translations of the Bible are not intended to be historically accurate translations but translations that place scripture in the specific context of the reader with the intention of helping the reader understand scriptural implications. His translation of Galatians is written to "The Letter to the Churches of the Georgia Convention."

13. Thieleman J. Van Braght, *The Bloody Theatre or Martyrs Mirror of the Defenseless Christians* (Scottdale, Pa.: Herald Press, 2001), p. 872.

14. William James, *Varieties of Religious Experience: A Study in Human Nature* (Toronto: Longmans, Green, and Co., 1925), 326-328.

15. Daniel Boyarin, *Dying For God: Martyrdom and The Making of Christianity and Judaism* (Stanford: Stanford University Press, 1999), 117.

16. Mark Jurgensmeyer, *Terror in the Mind of God*, 3rd. ed. (Berkeley: University of California Press, 2003), pp. 49-50.

17. Stanley Hauerwas and William H. Willimon, *Resident Aliens: Life in the Christian Colony* (Nashville: Abingdon Press, 1989), 36-48.

18. I write on this in deeper detail in the introduction to my *Living on Hope While Living in Babylon*, xi-xiv.

19. To take a preemptive strike against those who would commit the Marcionite heresy of suggesting that God was different (or it was a different God) in the Old Testament than in the New, Jesus, on multiple occasions, is clear that those who are not obedient to him will "depart . . . into the eternal fire prepared for the devil and his angels . . . and will go away into eternal punishment" (Matt. 25:41, 46).

20. The dollar bill claims that the United States represents a new order (*novus ordo*) in this world and that God favors this new order (*annuit coeptis*).

21. For a detailed account of Feuerbach's understanding of religion as a human creation and its implications for Christianity see Alister McGrath's *Christian Theology: An Introduction*, 4th. ed. (Oxford: Blackwell Publishing, 2007), 72, 174, 449-451.

22. Dietrich Bonhoeffer, *The Cost of Discipleship* (New York: The Macmillan Company, 1969), 99.

23. William Stringfellow, *An Ethic for Christians and Other Aliens in a Strange Land* (Eugene: Wipf & Stock Publishers, 2004), 13.

24. John Howard Yoder, *Concern: A Pamphlet Series for Christian Renewal* (No. 16, 1968), 18.

25. For a more thorough account of the development of this holiday, see James M. Loewen's *Lies My Teacher Told Me: Everything Your American History Textbook Got Wrong* (New York: New York Press, 1995), 67-89.

26. Ibid., 77.

27. Frank James, "Frank James' Speech," *Council of Interracial Books for Children Bulletin* 10.6 (1979), 13.

28. Abraham Lincoln, *Proclamation of Thanksgiving,* October 3, 1863.

29. In *Cloud of Witnesses*, ed. Jim Wallis and Joyce Hollyday, 81-89.

30. Stanley Hauerwas, *A Community of Character: Toward a Constructive Social Ethic* (Notre Dame: University of Notre Dame Press, 1981), 174.

31. Stanley Hauerwas, *Unleashing the Scriptures: Freeing the Bible from Captivity to America* (Nashville: Abingdon Press, 1993), 119.

32. Bertrand Russell, *Marriage and Morals* (New York: Liveright, 1957), 176.

33. To read his diatribe against Christendom see Soren Kierkegaard, *Attack Upon Christendom*, trans. Walter Lowe (Princeton, N.J.: Princeton University Press, 1991), 105-106.

# The Index

## U



## V



## W



## Y



## Z

# The Author

**TRIPP YORK** teaches in the Philosophy and Religion Department at Western Kentucky University. He has written numerous fiction and non-fiction books including *The Purple Crown: The Politics of Martyrdom, Living on Hope While Living in Babylon, The Devil Wears Nada,* and the children's book *Donkeys and Kings.*

York is also an actor and a lighting designer for the stage, having performed professionally in various states. Born in Burlington, North Carolina, he now lives in Bowling Green, Kentucky.

**CHUCK SEAY,** who developed the study guide for the book, is Pastor, Sheffield (Ala.) First Church of the Nazarene. He has a BA and an MA in Religion, both from Trevecca Nazarene University. He lives in Sheffield with his wife Jennifer and son Jackson.

CPSIA information can be obtained at www.ICGtesting.com
Printed in the USA
235716LV00003B/7/P